PRISON JOURNALS OF A PRIEST REVOLUTIONARY

By Philip Berrigan

Compiled and edited by Vincent McGee
Introduction by Daniel Berrigan

HOLT, RINEHART AND WINSTON
New York   Chicago   San Francisco

Prison Journals Of A Priest Revolutionary

Published simultaneously in Canada by Holt, Rinehart and Winston of Canada, Limited.

Library of Congress Catalog Card Number: 77–102136
First Edition

Designer: Marie Walborn
SBN: 03–084513–0
Printed in the United States of America

For those who die in war, and those who die opposing it. For the dead in Viet Nam: for Tom Merton and Dave Darst.

Contents

Editor's Note

In May, 1969, Philip Berrigan asked me to help prepare an account of his experience and thought during seven months of prison. A few articles written during the early stages of his confinement in Baltimore had been published as well as some reflections set down while awaiting trial and sentence for his crime—pouring blood on Selective Service files as an act against the Viet Nam war. These were only a beginning of the long period of contemplation and experience as a priest in prison, perhaps the first priest confined by the United States Government for a political crime against the State.

Not being content with his initial act, Phil Berrigan acted again just before his sentencing and this time home-made napalm replaced his blood as the agent of destruction of draft files.

Condemned to six years in prison and denied bail during appeal, Phil and Tom Lewis, a partner in both acts, were sent to the Federal Correctional Institutions at Lewisburg and Allenwood, Pennsylvania. Denied permission to write anything but letters to a selected list and carefully kept away from a typewriter, no articles appeared during their period in jail there.

After release on bail pending appeal on both the blood pouring and napalming, Phil wanted to put these months of thought and deep experience before the public. Kept on edge by the possibility of a quick return to prison and driven to put into print the account of jail, Phil turned to others to help bring this book into being.

The bulk of the text is taken from taped interviews and conversations during the late spring and early summer of 1969. Previously published articles (mostly from the Baltimore jail), transcripts from the Court record, and gleanings from many letters from Phil to his family, especially to his brother Daniel Berrigan, S.J., complete it.

I am grateful to Phil Berrigan for his trust and encouragement. I could not have given similar authority to another in the same task if the book was to be my own thoughts. Phil's desire to "get the message out" without exacting control over each sentence gives the lie to those who would dismiss his message as the ranting of an egomaniac determined to exploit an issue for publicity.

Francine du Plessix Gray helped throughout the work with valuable suggestions and critical assistance in the interviews. Joe Cunneen made the whole project real by his belief that it could and should be done and by quiet patience waiting for it to happen.

The Editors of Christianity and Crisis, The Catholic Worker, Liberation, and Fellowship kindly gave permission to print or excerpt articles originally in their publications.

Generous assistance was given in transcribing and typing the original drafts by Ellen Kaiderling and Jean McCoard and the final draft was typed by Lois Held.

Washington   VINCENT McGEE
January 10, 1970

THE BREAKING OF MEN and THE BREAKING OF BREAD: AN INTRODUCTION

On April 1, 1968, the trial of the "Baltimore Four" opened in the federal court of that city. David Eberhardt, Tom Lewis, Jim Mengel, and Phil Berrigan went on trial for pouring of blood on draft files in the Customs House in October of the previous year.

Three days prior to the opening of the trial, the government dropped the most serious of its charges, that of conspiracy. There remained three felony charges: hindering Selective Service operations, disrupting them, and destroying Selective Service records.

The night before the trial opened, President Johnson ordered his bombers home; no more forays over North Viet Nam. I remember how we received the news—as men who were accustomed only to bad news, suddenly and unexpectedly granted a breakthrough. It was as though we had surfaced with bursting lungs after a long and dangerous submersion. Indeed, the hope we were going on was a precarious resource. We seemed to be thrashing about, functioning without organs and limbs, our hearts almost ceasing to beat.

Then suddenly, a strange onset, a new emotion, so long absent from our lives so as to seem almost a myth. The President had stopped the bombing. Could Americans make it after all, racist and bellicose as we were?

Alas, alas. Johnson stalked off, a sullen marauder, recouping his losses as best he might. Kennedy died, McCarthy faded, Nixon came on; last year's Halloween was this year's political charade. The war goes on. For all we know at present writing, the incumbent and his palace court might bequeath the Viet Nam war, a mad national treasure, to a presidential successor in 1972, he to the next in line, and so on. For all we know, for all our scanning of the owlish eyes of Kissinger or the iron scowl of Mitchell, our leaders might see a new thing coming; a war in which the vets of 1965–69 will someday, from wheelchairs, send off their grandsons to bleed and let blood, for the sake of some fictive "finest national hour," under the aegis of some Asian bullyboy, thereafter to be hailed as "one of the two or three finest statesmen of the world."

And what of the impact of the war upon the Church? Officially speaking, in the Catholic instance, the sacred power has quite simply followed the secular, its sedulous ape. Bishops have blessed the war, in word and in silence. They have supplied chaplains to the military as usual and have kept their eyes studiously averted from related questions—ROTC on Catholic campuses, military installations, diocesan investments.

And yet, in a quite astonishing way, the war has shaken the church. Indeed, for the first time in the history of the American church, warfare has emerged as a question worthy of attention. A number of priests are in trouble on this deadly serious and secular issue. Consciences are shaken, the law of the land is being broken.

The good old definition of church renewal (everything in its place, children seen and not heard, virtue its own reward, a stitch in time, a bird in the hand, render unto Caesar) is shattered. The hope for strong, open, affectionate relationships between bishops and communities is dissipated. The war has deepened and widened the chasm; the bishops spoke too late and acted not at all. So the war, along with questions like birth control the survival of school systems, speech and its unfreedoms, control of properties and income, has made less and less credible official claims to superior wisdom and access to the divine will.

Which is not to say that the older game does not continue. It is merely to suggest that the older game is working badly. Once, when public affairs were more tranquil, peace was more easily kept at home. Grace was intoned at meals, authority was invoked. A common language prevailed. The paterfamilias could assure himself, on whatever occasion, whatever the subject, of a respectful hearing. But then, something happened. An intemperate father sent his son raging from the table. What happened, what in the world happened? A change of style, a trust broken, the difference between candor and the official line, between explaining the truth and explaining it away. Outcome: the family will never again know that easy and thoughtless unity which made it the very joy and pride of the culture.

The trial of the Baltimore Four is over, the sentence has been passed. Six years for Philip Berrigan and Tom Lewis, the chief protagonists. Catonsville followed, raining fire upon the files, a new instrument of destruction. Punishment also descended with all deliberate speed—concurrent sentences for Philip and Tom, 2½- and 3-year sentences for the others.

And the war went on, a Marat-Sade, Johnson-Nixon madhouse farce. There was no letup; we, and others like us, were in for it; a long, long push up Sisyphus Hill.

And yet, something else has happened. Since Catonsville, more hands than ours have stretched out, to block the brute gravity of that boulder. The Boston Two, the Milwaukee Fourteen, the D.C. Nine, the Pasadena Three, the Silver Springs Three, the Chicago Fifteen, the Women Against Daddy Warbucks, the New York Eight, the Boston Eight, the East Coast Conspiracy to Save Lives (the Philadelphia Eleven). Thus goes the current score; Mr. Nixon and his advisers and generals seem determined to extend it. Let the decision be theirs.

If there is one feature common to all the draft-file attacks, it is that they were invariably planned, and in major part executed, by Catholics. The fact is all the more remarkable, in face of the official stance of the church; in face also of the dissolution of the Left, broken by the repeated blows of national policy and factional despair. The Catholic community, that sturdy and well-fashioned hawk's nest, has suffered an invasion of doves; against all expectation, against nature and (they say) grace, a cross-breeding has followed.

Indeed, the Four of the Customs House—Mengel, Eberhardt, Lewis, and Berrigan—got something going. Their hands reached deeply into the springs of existence, cleared away the debris and filth, and set the pure waters running again. Some of us drank there, and took heart once more.

Maybe there was something to this Catholic tradition after all! We used to joke about it, in jail or out, reading our New Testament, breaking the Eucharist, battling to keep our perspective and good humor, trying with all our might to do something quite simple—to keep from going insane. Can it be that in this year, in this age of man, sanity requires so close a struggle? Is sanity so rare a resource on the American scene? Silone said once: It is difficult, but it is necessary, above all, to know who is insane and who is not.

Here are a few criteria.

It is madness to squander the world's resources on lethal military toys, while social misery and despair rise around a chorus of the damned.

It is madness to create the illusion of political or social change, all the while standing firm for spurious normalcy.

It is madness to renege on one's word, by activity which plays out the game one pretended to replace.

It is madness to ignore, with special savagery and determination, the viable and impassioned activists in our midst.

The madness goes on, it proliferates mightily. Behind a facade of sobriety and temperate action, the worst instincts of man are armed, rewarded, and set loose upon the world. An unthinkable Asian war, once a mere canker on the national body, a scratch on the tegument, undergone heedlessly and borne without second thought—it has festered and flowered, a wasting fever, a plague, a nightmare rushing into full day and again into night, and on and on for months and years, until only Jeremiah and Kafka could encompass its irrational horror.

The first trial of draft-file destroyers was that of the Baltimore Four. I remember it well, with the sharpness which a better and later mind always grants one. I sit once more in that musty, paneled courtroom, impersonal as a railroad station or a mortician's parlor. I see once more the back of my brother Philip's gray poll. The judge is droning on, angry and fretful, questioning the prospective jurors.

During World War II, I was tucked away in a seminary in the Maryland hills. We followed the war with maps and radios, a safe alternative. War raised no questions among us, it had no place in the sacred curriculum; we rejoiced and sorrowed and carried flags and paraded, even after Hiroshima. It was the worst conceivable method of transforming boys into men. Immunity from the grievous facts of modern war was part of an arrangement designed to keep us "pure" of bloodshed. In fact, the system did something else; it made us apt for complicity in an activity it purported to free us from. The source of our immunity was bad history; inevitably, it rendered us impure.

But we were to learn the truth later; and even then, only a few of us learned it at all.

Philip fought in World War II. He was a soldier's soldier, decorated and commissioned in the European theater.

One prospective juror at his trial was an old lady; her son was a chaplain in the armed forces. The judge asked, "Would you be capable of coming to an unbiased conclusion in this case?" She answered, "I would, with the help of God."

It became clearer, as the jurors were questioned, how nearly impossible it was to come upon an American who was not, in some tragic and real way, through relatives or friends or emotional bias, involved in the war game. Wars—World I, World II, Korean, Vietnamese, Cold, Hot—the choices were rich, a technological feast.

After his ordination, Philip spent several years in ghetto parishes and schools in Washington, New Orleans, and Baltimore. He was undergoing a kind of boot-camp training, the creation of a dedicated activist. From the beginning, he stood with the urban poor. He rejected the traditional, isolated stance of the Church in black communities. He was also incurably secular; he saw the Church as one resource, bringing to bear on the squalid facts of racism the light of the Gospel, the presence of inventive courage and hope. He worked with CORE, SNCC, the Urban League, the forms of Catholic action then in vogue. He took Freedom Rides, did manual work of all kinds, begged money and gave it away, struggled for scholarships for black students.

Six years in New Orleans; then he was appointed to the seminary staff of the Josephite Fathers at Newburgh, New York. The war had broken into fury. The Hudson Valley, racist to its bones, primed by the Birchers and the Minutemen, proud of its infamous Newburgh mayor, was in no mood to grant equal time, or any time at all, to a peacenik priest. Who did he think he was, anyway? Forty miles down the river, Most Reverend Spellman was girding on his buckler like a vestment, invoking Don John of Austria. Now, there was a man who made sense, and a cardinal at that! Philip's fate was not long in doubt—the toe end of the military boot. The night he left for a new job in the Baltimore ghetto, we held a party to celebrate the publication of his first book, *No More Strangers*.

He started over. He was incapable of meanness of spirit, even in dark hours, and wasted no time licking his wounds. He set about organizing in the inner city. Housing was the main issue locally; so was the war, for the poor were the first victims of the roundup. In all the troubled days that followed, I remember how the poor people stood with him and with his friends.

The Vatican Council found him only mildly interested. And I think now, in the light of all we have endured since, how correct his detachment was; no illusions made for no disillusion. Both he and I were cooled, I think, by our sense of the pervasive cultural illness of the American Church, its illusions about moral superiority, its massive victimization by racism, by cold- and hot-war fervor, by anticommunism. We suspected that the Council would offer only a limited kind of help. Those who were acting on the assumption of instant change from Rome were bound, someday, and soon, to be put down hard.

Philip was nobody's fool. He knew, through his own suffering, the difference between pronunciamentos and performance. The poor had conferred on him that wisdom which sees, and sees through, the big talk of little minds. His own mind was too lively and encompassing to be bemused by the rhetoric of totalists or tokenists—whether of church or of state.

His gifts began to flower in New Orleans. He was, as I came to realize, a good, even an impassioned speaker. He did his homework and wrote well. He was carrying forward an old tradition in our family, of making noise and being congenitally unhappy with false peace and wrong-headed power.

I sat in court; my brother was a defendant; it was a new scene for priests. And I thought of the delicious logic which had brought him to such a place. The war would continue, other priests would be drawn into trouble. But Philip was the first. As far as we can discover, he was the first priest to be tried for a political crime, to be convicted and imprisoned. (He and Tom Lewis served seven months after the trial of the Catonsville Nine. Bail was finally granted them in December of 1968.)

I sat in that courtroom, still a spectator. And I thought how inconceivable it was that Philip should have been spared. For he is free, lucid, and fearless. He is a public man who chooses his issues, one or two at a time, one or two in a lifetime. He would say that if the issue is the right one, one issue is enough. It will lead one to all the others.

But what of our brothers, the American Catholic community? Who will lead them, and in what direction? For most of them, the war years have been a kind of Dantesque twilight. Nothing is clear. Phantoms and demons mingle, men and trees; no great evil, no great good. Normalcy and numbers are the game. Catholics fit into the cultural landscape so neatly that Kennedy or Johnson or Nixon could fairly count on us for a Sunday blessing in a typical, filthy week of war.

Philip is something else. And this is why Philip stood in that courtroom, stood again with the Nine at Cantonsville. It is why he stood with us for a third time, equally angry, equally helpless, for a travesty conducted on duplicate charges by the state of Maryland in June of 1969. Three trials, a few resisting men, a war that wheels around us, coherant as a solar system, implacable as the gods of violence, long gone in madness.

I finish these notes in the autumn of 1969. "Men had hoped," writes Brecht, "that someday there might be bread to eat. Now they hope that someday there may be stones to eat." Stones for bread; it is the reversal of the old biblical temptation. Everything we used to call hope is gone.

But this may be exactly the moment we were hoping for, in spite of all. For despair is not a proper word to apply to this man Philip, or to his friends. Indeed, it is a time of the breaking of men. And yet one hears, in such lives, in such hands, in a courtroom where justice is corrupted and the innocent stand in ordeal, the sound of the breaking of bread.

Daniel Berrigan

I'm not at all clear about what to call this; in fact, I have no definite idea of the form my writing in jail will take. It will not be a diary, nor will I be writing what should rightly be called meditations or reflections. Simply an unconventional look at the world through the mirror of prison life. Hopefully, a Christian look.

A title is unimportant, and can be left to others. What is important is why I am in prison, what prison life signifies for a Christian, and what it may indicate for the future.

Jail for me was an entirely voluntary affair, one of the predictable consequences connected with serious political dissent. This is not to say that I chose jail, or preferred it, but only that I felt civil disobedience was a Christian duty, and accepted jail as a consequence.

In any event, there will be others like me, and as a priest perhaps I can offer other clerics a service comparable to that offered our young men by the David Millers, the Tom Cornells, and other young Americans jailed because of their opposition to war.

But why should I expect Catholic priests to be leaders in this form of witness? It seems at least that some elusive and mysterious influences are converging in this direction. Certainly, Vatican II is "at fault," with its emphasis on free-

dom of conscience; so is the civil-rights movement and its nonviolent philosophy. Always in the background has been the long preparation of the ground by the Catholic Worker movement and its undeviating concern for the poor, for black people, and its "yes" to the world of justice, freedom, and peace. There is also the challenge provided by American young people, and their insistence on values the Church should champion, but seldom does. And, of course, the menacing aspect of world events has become increasingly difficult for any serious person to ignore. Another positive factor—which Church liberals generally ignore—is the freedom made possible by clerical celibacy. Finally, we should also take note of the two-edged absolutism of Catholic discipline; it produces, admittedly, many human casualties, but can it not also provide the training ground for saints and heroes?

Philip Berrigan

PRISON JOURNALS OF A PRIEST REVOLUTIONARY

CAN WE SERVE
BOTH LOVE AND WAR?

Sanford Gottlieb, the political-action director of SANE, is one of the most informed men in America on the Viet Nam war, and he often gives lectures on the subject. During the question period after one such talk before a predominantly Christian audience, a somewhat antagonistic questioner arose to challenge him.

"Mr. Gottlieb," he began, "you seem to know all the answers. What do we do about this war?"

"Before trying to answer that," Gottlieb said, "can I ask you a question or two?"

"Go ahead," said the man.

"Are you a Christian?"

"Sure," came the reply, "and proud of it."

"Fine," said Gottlieb. "Now, I happen to believe that Jesus Christ was the world's greatest revolutionary, because he loved his enemies, and commanded his followers to love their enemies. I believe this and I try to live it, though I

1

myself am a Jew. My question, therefore, is: Do you believe it?"

"Sure, I believe it," answered the man. "But you didn't answer my question. I asked you what we should do about this war."

"That's your problem!" said Gottlieb.

The man sat down angry, unnerved, and quite confused.

Our poor friend's dilemma is, in fact, the dilemma of this country—in Viet Nam, in the arms race, and in the world. Most Christians and most Americans have great difficulty in seeing the I (the self) as being the we (humanity). Consequently, we cannot feel the effects of our actions as other people feel them, we cannot see ourselves as others see us. And so, by and large, we think we can have peace by fighting wars, we think we can rape a people and have them love us, we think, by way of practical norm, that we can have everything that wealth and arms can force from others. Or nearly everything. Most children could tell us, I suppose (provided they have not played with too many war toys or watched too many Westerns), that you can't have war and peace at once and that, given the determination of the Vietnamese, you can't have a truce in Viet Nam and a base against China. One or the other has to go.

To go a bit further into the "problem," we cannot ravage the ecology of Viet Nam and kill ten civilians for every soldier and expect to have anything but "do-or-die" opposition. We cannot bomb North Viet Nam and support U Thant's program for peace. We cannot replace Polaris with Poseidon and expect to avoid an arms-race escalation into ABM systems. We cannot manipulate encephalitis and yellow fever for person-to-person transmission and have other men trust us. We cannot have the Pentagon owning fifty-three percent of all federal property and have civilian control of government and diplomacy. We cannot fight the

abstraction of communism by killing the men who believe
in it. We cannot propagandize for peace while our deeds
give the lie to our words. In a word, we can't have it both
ways. And that's why our friend and so many Christians
and Americans have a "problem." How can we serve love
and war? The fact is that we can't.

People have, I would say, two problems when they try
to serve love. The first is to know themselves; the second
is to know what they must be. As to the first, we are, in
effect, a violent people and none of the mythological pabu-
lum fed us at Mother's knee, in the classroom, or at Fourth
of July celebrations can refute the charge. The evidence is
too crushing, whether it be Hiroshima, or nuclear equiva-
lents of seven tons of TNT for every person on this planet,
or scorched earth in the Iron Triangle, or Green Berets in
Guatemala, or subhuman housing in the ghettos of America.
A substantial share of our trouble comes from what we own,
and how we regard what we own. President Johnson told
our troops: "They [the rest of the world] want what we have
and we're not going to give it to them." To prevent them,
one thing needs to be done: "Bring home the coonskin and
hang it on the wall."

On December 29, 1966, Secretary of State Dean Rusk
talked about the prospects for a Gross National Product of
eight hundred billion dollars in 1967, the implication being
that possession of such wealth destines America to be the
international arbiter of justice. What Johnson and Rusk are
talking about is this: we control about fifty-two percent of
the world's productive wealth. In 1965, General Motors'
sales of twenty-one billion dollars exceeded the Gross National Product of all but nine other nations. In 1966, it may
have been all but seven, but in any case, one-sixteenth of
the world's population controls half of its wealth. That is
why, I suppose, Reinhold Niebuhr recently said that we

are in Viet Nam to protect a policy of economic imperialism. He was saying nothing startling or new. President Eisenhower said it in 1953:

> Now let us assume that we lost Indo-China. . . . The tin and tungsten that we so greatly value from that area would cease coming. . . . So when the U.S. votes 400 million dollars to help that war, we are not voting a give-away program. We are voting for the cheapest way that we can to prevent the occurrence of something that would be of a most terrible significance to the United States of America, our security, our power and ability to get certain things we need from the riches of Indo-Chinese territory and from Southeast Asia.

And Henry Cabot Lodge said it in 1965:

> Geographically, Viet Nam stands at the hub of a vast area of the world—Southeast Asia—an area with the population of 249 million persons. . . . He who holds or has influence in Viet Nam can affect the future of the Philippines and Formosa to the East, Thailand and Burma with their huge rice surpluses to the west, and Malaysia and Indonesia with their rubber, ore and tin to the south. . . . Viet Nam does not exist in a geographical vacuum—from it large storehouses of wealth and population can be influenced and undermined.

ECONOMICS OF WAR

Ideologically, we are in Viet Nam because of China; economically, we are there because of wealth. Ideology has been tailored to fit economic aggrandizement. Scripture tells us that one must choose God or riches. This nation has overwhelmingly made its choices, and it is riches. Our shrinking world being what it is, we are now in the process of assuring the same status quo abroad as at home, and that means keeping the "haves" on top and the "have nots" on the bottom. Foreign policy is increasingly becoming indistinguishable from domestic policy. The curtain is no longer iron or bamboo or cotton, it is mostly dollar and to a lesser extent ruble, franc, and pound. Abroad, the "have nots" are two billion people, most of them brown, yellow, or black; at home, we have thirty-four million poor people, fourteen million of whom are black. The arguments that we are in South Viet Nam to ensure the freedom of that people, that we are bombing the North to make a rising "quotient of pain" the price of aggression in the South, that behind the National Liberation Front stands Hanoi, and behind Hanoi, Peking, represents a degree of hypocrisy unmatched in history. They are pure cold-war rhetoric. The only present freedom we're fighting for is our own, and that is of questionable value, since ultimately it means the right to stay on top of the anthill and fight off those crawling up the slopes.

When a people arbitrarily decides that this planet and its riches are to be divided unequally among equals, and that the only criterion for the division is the amount of naked power at its disposal, diplomacy tends to be essentially military, truth tends to be fiction, and the world tends to become a zoo without benefit of cages. And war tends to be the ultimate rationality, because reason has been bankrupted of human alternatives.

This tells us something about what we are economically and politically, if not personally. And yet the personal integrity of each one of us is indissolubly linked with our social integrity; in truth, the two cannot be separated. This means that it is useless to oppose the violence in Viet Nam while refusing to face personal violence in its every manifestation: bias, arrogance, insensitivity, dislikes, indiscriminate sensuality, trivial values.

By the same token, it is useless to condemn such a war

while neglecting to hold one's representatives in Congress to a reasonable position, or while gaining one's livelihood from war industry. What I'm trying to say is this: Our lives, to be agencies of peace, must stand the scrutiny of both God and man, and by man I mean not our peers, but the billions of people suffering from war, tyranny, starvation, disease, and the burden of color prejudice. In our better moments we may pity them, but sentiment has yet to stop bombing or feed starving children. They will hold us to our acts, and if these acts will not bear human analysis, we will be judged and condemned and withstood in the same coin.

If disengagement from the violent aspects of the "system" is one side of peacemaking, service of truth and human rights is the other. As Pope John used to say, "Love ought to be the motive, but justice the object." This is a very large order, calling for people who know humanity by principle and by experience, who are as pained by the plight of starving millions in India as by the sufferings of our own poor, by Chase Manhattan Bank investments in South Africa as by the ruthlessness of Detroit car manufacturers, by napalmed Vietnamese children as by rat-bitten Harlem kids. For as they see it, people are one before they are many, they are man before men, not objects to be manipulated, exploited cursed, or killed. As for themselves, they know what it is to be a minority but are not disconcerted by it, for, with Thoreau, they know that being right is being a majority of one. They are confident, too, in their faith, knowing that God has chosen the weak things of this world to confound the strong, and that the focal point of divine action is always a tiny remnant of the faithful. They know, finally, that politicians will not have the final say, nor will technologists, or Joint Chiefs of Staff, or war industrialists, or churchmen who bless war with the Gospel. They are the people who when asked, "Do you believe in the revolution of Jesus Christ?" will be able to answer yes, whether their faith springs from the Jewish prophets or the Gospel, or Muhammad, or contemporary humanism. When they are told, "That's your problem," they will answer heartily, "You're right, it is." And they will then go out and do something about it.

STATEMENT
AT SENTENCING,
MAY 24, 1968

I am grateful to the judge and to this court for the opportunity to speak. Mr. Lewis and I, while under conviction and awaiting sentence, have acted once more against the apparatus of war. And for that, many people have judged us "irresponsible," or "untrustworthy." One prominent and respected friend called us "a danger to the community." A remark we accept with equanimity, if not pain, since we feel our friend has the equipment to understand better.

One acts as we did because of a certain view of man, and of man's world. We claim to be Christian, but that is a claim never really verified or completed. It is rather a process of becoming, since man is by definition one who becomes himself—a painful but glorious process, as history tells us. In the same context, we believe that God's son became man so that man might become himself—which is to say, a son of the Father, a brother to the Son, a temple of God's Spirit, a brother to all other brothers. Becoming a man, we feel, is becoming what Christ was. And this we have tried to do.

When one deals with man, therefore, one deals with the Body of the Savior, a Body for which God died, and in which He still suffers. One does not deal with it lightly or irresponsibly—it is a sacred thing illumined by truth, nourished and built up by love, served by justice, and it must be protected against injustice.

So much for man. What of man's world? By way of brutal analogy, it is more a jungle than a human community. Fifty million men died in World War II, vast areas of Eurasia and Japan were reduced to a smoking rubble, atomic weapons were used, a fateful precedent, just because it was a precedent. And with the ink of armistice wet, and with the slaughter and terror of World War II apparently forgotten as a lesson, the West moved into the cold war, or as some call it, the first stage of World War III.

Since 1945, the nations have spent over a trillion dollars on weapons, which is, in breakdown, a million-million dollars. The five nuclear powers now have the capability of, conservatively, thirty times overkill—or cinderizing this planet thirty times over. Tiny and obscure nations buy arms before they undertake development or offer their people bread; they buy arms mostly from the great powers, who have a special interest in seeing them weak, neocolonial, and client. Atomic war has been narrowly avoided five or six times, while great-power atomic accidents, dozens in number, could have provided the spark igniting world nuclear holocaust.

To further complicate such appalling madness, humanity is divided along caste and racial lines—the "have" and "have-not" polarity. The "haves," one-third of mankind, are mostly white, mostly North-Atlantic, and they control in excess of eighty percent of the world's wealth and productive capacity, while the "have-nots," two-thirds of humanity, over two billion people, either starve or are caught in the fierce throes of revolution against the white world. In fact, many students of the world scene say that the Communist-Capitalist struggle is a side drama to something immeasurably more significant and profound—a race war of global dimensions.

Americans, we feel, must face realities like these if there is to be any turn toward hope. Our country now stands at the pinnacle of world power—we are history's most powerful empire, and perhaps its most dangerous one. We are richer than all the rest of mankind, and our military power surpasses that of all the rest of mankind. The equation between the two, wealth and military power, is not an idle one.

Meanwhile, the problems of empire plague us and drive us into profound anxiety and unrest. Our intervention in Viet Nam is illegal according to our own Constitution and according to international law. And by the best appraisal, unwinnable short of nuclear war. Thailand and Laos are now aflame, while a dozen Latin-American countries smolder. In the Middle East, we composedly sell arms to both sides, in the apparent hope that the Arabs and Israelis will wear each other out with profit to us, and without involving the Russians and ourselves in something more serious.

What is the domestic side of empire? What some call the Second American Revolution—our poor marching on Washington as national wealth reaches unprecedented heights; our ghettos boiling with unresolved frustration and rage; our youth in revolt against academic life and military conscription; while a quiet and unreported rebellion brews among our servicemen. As one informed person told me, "Every American brig and stockade in the world is bulging with GIs refusing to fight in Viet Nam."

To what central cause can one attribute such enormous

dissent and resistance? The power structure calls it a breakdown of law and order, but those who resist say it stems from a breakdown of law and justice. Which is to say—their conclusion is essentially the same as that of those resisting abroad. Both feel that the American power structure is, by and large, lawless, and that it must be made lawful.

Why "lawless"? "Unjust" or "violent" would do as well for description. But whatever word is useful to describe our nation's plight, we ask today in this court: What is lawful about a foreign policy which allows economic control of whole continents, which tells the Third World, as it tells our black people, "You'll make it sometime, but only under our system, at the pace we decide, by dole, by handout, by seamy charity, by delayed justice." Don't try it any other way! What is lawful about peace under a nuclear blanket, the possible penetration of which impels our leaders to warn us of one hundred million American casualties? What is lawful about Viet Nam, more and more Americans dead and wounded, plus our implacable intent to ruin irreparably a people and their country? What is lawful about building warmaking into our economy, to the extent that warmaking is our main production—to the extent, indeed, that our military establishment now has such political power that we no longer know if it can be controlled? What is lawful about war profiteering, which Admiral Rickover claims exceeds four billion a year? What is lawful about the rich becoming richer, and the poor poorer, in this country or abroad? By what right do the powerful gather about the public trough, only to consume others, and to destroy themselves by indulgence?

These are not times for building justice; these are times for confronting injustice. This, we feel, is the number-one item of national business—to confront the entrenched, massive, and complex injustice of our country. And to confront it justly, nonviolently, and with maximum exposure of oneself and one's future.

Like the other defendants, I am an American and a Christian insofar as I face my country and humanity under the Declaration of Independence and the Gospel. As a democratic man, I must cling to a tradition of protest going back to our birth as a nation—traditions which brightened our finest hours as people. Jefferson, Washington, Madison, Thoreau, Emerson, Whitman, and Twain; they also stand in the dock today; they judge you as you judge me. They judge our uses of political power, our racism, our neglect of the poor, our courts serving the interests of war. I do not hesitate to assert that were these men alive today, they would disobey as I have disobeyed and be convicted as I am convicted.

As a Christian, I must love and respect all men—loving the good they love, hating the evil they hate. If I know what I am about, the brutalization, squalor, and despair of other men demeans me and threatens me if I do not act against its source. This is perhaps why Tom Lewis and I acted again with our friends. The point at issue with us was not leniency or punishment, nor courage or arrogance, not being a danger to the community or a benefit to it—but what it means to be a democratic man and a Christian man. And if we provide the slightest light upon those two momentous questions, it is enough for us.

America can at this point treat us as it wills. If it can find justice for us and for the growing millions of citizens who refuse complicity in its crimes, then it will display a stamina of reform in full accordance with its national creed. If it cannot find justice for us, then its cup of violence will fill up and up, finally to brim over. And at that mysterious point, we defendants will have been proven right in choosing revolution over reform.

Personally, I have little doubt as to the decision this court will take in the name of our country. But whatever the outcome today, I stand where stand I must—for my country and for my family, here and abroad.

LETTER FROM A BALTIMORE JAIL

There was no conspiracy, as the government suspected. There was only a group of friends, trying to validate themselves as a community, by a decision for peace.

I make no pretension in calling this a "Letter from a Baltimore Jail." Many of you remember Martin Luther King's "Letter from a Birmingham Jail." Together we cherish the man and the martyr. As I recall, Dr. King's letter silenced his critics, most of whom were Christians and some of whom were Catholics. I do not intend that, nor do I hope for it. I ask you merely to ponder events with me and then to make whatever response you choose. As our President says, "Let us reason together." So, a letter from a Baltimore jail, written with all the esteem and love I can muster.

Many of you have been sorely perplexed with me (us); some of you have been angry, others despairing. (One parishioner writes of quarreling with people who thought me mad.) After all, isn't it impudent and sick for a grown man

14

(and a priest) to slosh blood—wasn't it duck's blood—on draft files; to terrorize harmless secretaries doing their job; to act without ecclesiastical permission and to disgrace the collar and its sublime office? And then, while convicted and awaiting sentence, to insult a tolerant government by bursting wildly into another draft board with a larger troop of irresponsibles—forcibly seizing the records, forcibly carrying them outside, there to burn them with napalm? With smiles and jubilation? Disgusting, frenzied, violent; many of you wrote or told us that.

You had trouble with blood as a symbol—uncivilized, messy, bizarre. *Time, Newsweek,* and the Catholic Church lent their impressive authority. You had trouble with the war —had it really gotten so bad that men had to do that? You had trouble with departures from legitimate dissent, from law and order itself. You had trouble with napalm as a symbol—what's that got to do with it? You had trouble with us calling violence nonviolence, and the press calling nonviolence violence. You had trouble with destruction of property; with civil disobedience; with priests getting involved, and getting involved this much. Let's face it: Perhaps half of you had trouble with us acting at all.

You'll forgive me for interpreting, but it has a certain legitimacy here. My friends and I have had long dealings with the press, and we think it generally reflects the attitudes of the people. We have read our mail and have spoken to—and listened to—hundreds of audiences around the country. We have talked to congressmen, cabinet members, military and intelligence men in Washington, and to state and local officials. We have spoken to servicemen on trains, buses, and planes; we have written to relatives in Viet Nam. We have experienced war firsthand, several of us; we have served Church and country abroad, several of us. And one of us (my brother) spent a week in Laos and another in Viet Nam negotiating the release of three American fliers. We have learned, finally, from the peace movement—its rhetoric, aims, convictions, criticisms of us. Pardon us for interpreting.

Let me share with you an analogy to introduce mutual concerns. Imagine, if you will, a tiny community of sixteen people, relatively isolated, exclusive, and self-sufficient. Its leader is leader for the simple reason that he owns more than the rest put together. Because he does, the others work for him, making him richer as they make themselves poorer. Naturally there is fear on his part, discontent on the others'. The rich man hires guards and intelligence; he resolves to protect his person and property. He often exhorts them, telling them of the honor of their role, carefully avoiding terms like "mercenary" and "spy." When unrest develops, it is ferreted out, condemned as godless, subversive, and hostile to law and order. Then it is crushed.

A WEALTHY AND POWERFUL NATION

Another analogy, if you please. A nation that counts its wealth in dollars had two billionaires, six half-billionaires, and 153 multimillionaires with more than one hundred million each. Paradoxically, this nation had also many poor— ten million who hungered, twenty million inadequately fed. Many of the rich, thinking undoubtedly of other services to the nation, pay no taxes, while the poor pay upwards of fourteen percent (I must banish this dirty thought resolutely: If the rich do not draft the law, they certainly apply it!) And the citizens' attitude toward dollars is so curious that in their land of freedom and equality, five percent of the people control twenty percent of the wealth; at the other end, twenty percent control five percent. And that's what somebody calls the symmetry of injustice.

Need I remind you that my clumsy analogies depict—as through a glass darkly—our beloved country, abroad and at home? Need I remind you that wealth can be legislated

abroad—NATO, SEATO, CENTO, OAS—as it is at home
in graduated income tax, oil-depletion allowance? And if
legislation fails, unrest can be militarized: Viet Nam, the
Dominican Republic, Newark, Detroit. Need I remind you
that wealth is such a priority with us that we both add to
it by war production (defense budget, eighty billion dollars
plus) and protect it by war (Viet Nam, Thailand, Laos,
Guatemala, Bolivia, Peru)?

Need I remind you that the United States maintains its
wealth by an imperial economy—foreign investments total-
ing seventy billion dollars in 1967, eighty percent of all the
foreign investments in the world? (Another dirty thought
that I must banish resolutely: Empires have always valued
power more than wisdom, survival more than justice.)

Need I remind you that law legislated for the few equals
lawlessness for the many, and that lawlessness rests not so
much on crime in the streets as on crimes at the top? Need
I remind you that conscription reflects national injustice
more than the ghetto, simply because it plays a more deadly
deceit upon its victims. "Tell my soldiers what they really
fight for," said Frederick the Great, "and the ranks would
be empty in the morning."

As for the blood, it was ours: the FBI made sure of that.
Our greatest mistake was technical incompetence, not getting
enough of it. You showed an odd fascination with blood,
my friends. You worried the point as a puppy worries a
rubber bone, and with as much profit. Surely men foolhardy
enough to do such a stunt would be foolhardy enough to
take their own blood?

We were painfully educated by people concentrating on
blood while neglecting its meaning. Blood is life—the Bible
says so; lose enough or shed enough, and death results.
Blood is redemption (freedom) also, depending on how it
is shed; the contrast between Cain and Christ shows that.
Our point was simply this: We could claim no right to life

or freedom as long as the Viet Nam war—U Thant calls it one of the most barbarous in history—deprives Americans and Vietnamese of life and freedom. If we said no to the war, we could say yes to its victims, and to sharing their predicament.

What of official disobedience, you wonder, and disgrace to the priesthood? The answer depends on one's frame of reference, I suppose. Is a Christian Christ's man, or the state's; is the Church a community of belief or a spiritual spa? If the first in both cases, I have honored the priesthood and have been obedient to the Church. One must deal, it seems, with two realities—the Church as Christ's body, and the Church as the body of man. Which has the higher reality? If you say the first, then the first must be the benchmark, and the other found and served. One cannot interpret Christ by interpreting man. One rather says what man can be because of what Christ is.

You claim we disregard legitimate dissent at the expense of law and order. Quite the contrary. My brother and I have had experience with legitimate dissent for ten years, the Melvilles nearly as long in Guatemala, Tom Lewis and David Eberhardt nearly as long. We have seen legitimate dissent first ridiculed, then resisted, then absorbed. To become, in effect, an exercise in naïveté.

THE USELESSNESS OF LEGITIMATE DISSENT

If society can absorb lawlessness, or protests against lawlessness, without redress, it suggests its own insensitivity to injustice. Law and order tend to become a figment because law and justice become harder to attain. With ineffectual grievance machinery, there is little hope of redress. Which may explain why legal scholars say the Constitution must allow civil disobedience to check itself in keeping with the balance it constructs among the three branches of the federal government.

In point of fact, we have experienced intimately the uselessness of legitimate dissent. The war grows in savagery, more American coffins come home, Vietnamese suffering would seem to have passed the limits of human endurance. Astute and faithful men, including congressional doves, say we can't win in Viet Nam without World War III. Others disagree, saying that World War III has begun, that it is merely a question of time before one side or the other employs nuclear weapons. We have nuclear weapons in Viet Nam; we have carried them over the Chinese mainland; China is a nuclear power; Russia and China have not dissolved their mutual-defense treaty. These are not debatable items by either side.

In face of these facts, for some Americans to ask others to restrict their dissent to legal channels is asking them to joust with a windmill. More than that, it is to ask them for silent complicity with unimaginable injustice, for political unrepresentation, for voicelessness in the fate that threatens everyone. God would never ask that of any man; no man can ask it justly of other men.

In turn, we destroyed property; indeed, the people's property. Ah, there's the rub. The Jews had their golden calf, Americans have their own property. Its misuse and disparity is our most sinister social fact; its international purusit has brought us to grips with the world. Scripture calls the love of money the root of all evil, a judgment true enough to require respectful attention. The Lord said that renouncing possessions and following Him were the two criteria of discipleship, so mutually reliant in fact that the absence of one cancels the other. In contrast, no people have cherished and celebrated property as we have, even to the point of obsessions and orgy.

Americans would not quarrel with destroying German gas ovens or the Nazi and Stalinist slave camps. We would not quarrel with violent destruction of war matériel threatening us. But let the issue become nonviolent destruction of "weapons for defense"—hydrogen bombs; germ cultures at Fort Detrick, Maryland, cluster-bomb units, Stoner rifles, Selective Service files—and the issue suffers an abortive death. Americans know, with a kind of avaricious instinct, that property like this serves as insurance policy to private property. As our President says, "They want what we have, and we're not going to give it to them."

Friends, countrymen, such is our case. It may be over-assertive and presumptuous in spots. That is for you to judge. But here it is, and here we take our stand, because, obviously, it is the best one we have. Disagree as you might, one thing you must acknowledge—our stand disrupts our lives, removes our liberty, exiles us for a considerable time from our friends, our communities, our country, our church —from everything we love so passionately. What of your stand? It costs most of you neither risk nor loss, except perhaps your integrity, your country's welfare, your Christianity. Perhaps your immediate gain may be your long-term loss.

In closing, there is one request we make. We can fairly predict that our government will show flexible leniency if we prove ourselves contrite. We can't be contrite at this point, not seeing reasons to be so. For you to point out our errors firmly and patiently would be a great service, truly in the spirit of the Gospel. It could restore to us confidence in our government and our church, and could return us to our families, friends, and assignments. It could as well allow us a constructive part in building the Great Society—instead of a destructive share in tearing it down. In all humanity, we plead for your help.

Love and peace and gratitude

In Christ

Fr. Philip Berrigan, S.S.J.

A COMMUNITY OF NINE

"They're in better spirits than those of us on the outside!" *The Baltimore Sun* of May 19 quoted Fred Weisgal, our lawyer, to this effect. We howled in glee at the remark, because it seemed true to us. And because true, full of irrepressible human ironies. The awareness struck us then, as before, that authority—both government and Church—had far more problems than we.

For one thing, we had the government upset by resting our case on the Declaration of Independence, which we judged as fine a political expression of the Gospel as exists. Power and privilege required the hypocrisy of the government professing to support the Declaration—a pure expression of self-determination—while living social and economic Darwinism. And legal reaction against us came purely from our attempts to illustrate such political schizophrenia. A political house divided against itself, and thinking that Johnson's consensus would alone save it from crashing down.

Moreover, we embarrassed the Church in terms of its own profession and rhetoric. Try as it might, the Church cannot

entirely kill the Gospel or its Christ. It will always possess
an inner dynamic rebelling against wedding with the powers
of this world. When my superior threatens me with ecclesiastical sanctions for confronting a warmaking society, he is
not speaking of the Gospel's death, but more of institutional
bankruptcy.

But to return to the original point, we have the apparent
problems—political and Church authority. Three priests are
in official disgrace; the other Catholics in our group are
ignored simply because canonical jurisdiction offers no ready
weapon against them. Church bureaucrats—if my superior
is in any way typical—would prefer better redress against
us. But since they are at a loss in this, they leave heavier
duties of punishment to the government, contenting themselves meanwhile with bluster and threats of removal. Take
it as an axiom: For American bureaucracies survival is their
corporate version of self-interest. And they will react to
stimuli upon nerve ends or to body blows upon viscera with
the same outpouring of defensive rectitude. One is rewarded
by the priceless experience of seeing them once more as
they are.

In any event, Christian communities form today under
pressure of events and around the issues which prompt the
events. We have such a community here in Baltimore County
Jail—diverse, rich, intelligent, loving. And tough. One hesi-
tates to use that word, but these are persons who have been
molded by human suffering, including their own. One does
not undertake realistically the cause of exploited people
without facing oneself and the whole galaxy of personal
fears and weaknesses.

Others have remarked to us from time to time of our
"courage" or "lack of fear." Their observations, we feel, are
superficial and misleading. In any human equation, the
difference between us and them is not the absence or presence of fear, but perhaps in facing up to it. When people

look at the dark recesses of American society, and understand more fully its ambiguous and entrenched genius, its
enormous capacity for violence and exploitation, its anxiety
and retaliatory power, they stimulate fear and know—perhaps for the first time—public despair.

More specifically, when most Americans realize that
bureaucracies of government, business, and church have
gulped them down whole and intact, where anonymity is
their name and where function becomes almost cellular
maintenance and reproduction, they tend to be overwhelmed
by their helplessness and to retreat to a womblike confidence
in the system. Indeed, few Americans understand how both
the capitalistic and Soviet technocracies make people as
mass-produced as assembly-line productions, with about
as few options. In effect, people begin to resemble the
products they consume: The system digests them, they di-
gest its products.

To return to our community, there are three priests, three
married people, one Christian Brother, three laymen. If
that gets confusing, Father Tom Melville is married and a
priest, despite his excommunication and suspension. So he
considers himself, and so we consider him. If the Melville
presence in jail is any indication, their marriage has lent
fruitful dimensions to their Christian ministry. To be ejected
from Guatemala for identifying with the poor there, to be
the brunt of ecclesiastical rejection and punishment, to risk
beating or death or return to the United States, and then to
attack nonviolently the injustice of this society in its "rich
man's war, poor man's fight" system of conscription, is to add
a modest dimension to Christian ministry.

David Darst is our Christian Brother from Saint Louis,
who teaches in a black high school there. We had restive
suspicions of David at first, simply because we could not
understand why he would join us in serious civil disobedience without being involved in the Resistance. Slightly

paranoid about security, because of previous experience of our "free" society, we had suspicions of him as a religious "snoop," whose superpatriotism might have led him to infiltrate us for some branch of federal or military intelligence. But our fears were allayed; David had resisted the draft and had refused induction in Saint Louis on April 4, a stand unique among religious brothers, taken against considerable opposition and with only desultory support. David, we think, is quite too good to be true.

Authorities here have separated the women, putting them upstairs—in fact, it is policy not to allow them to Sunday Eucharist with the men. Marge Melville and Mary Moylan are exceptional people—women of strength, balance, and good humor. From time to time we succumb to the temptation of comparing them with more knowledgeable and experienced human-rights people—women and men—to the considerable expense of the latter.

Marge's fourteen years in Guatemala as a Maryknoll nun had led her into the student movement, and from there to concern for the peasants and the need for revolution. Mention of self-defense to the peasants is enough to get one expelled in a country like Guatemala—precisely what happened to Marge and Tom and John Hogan.

Mary has been back from Africa some two years, where she served as a nurse with the Women's Volunteer Association. Named director of the association, she made its headquarters in Washington a center of human activity and concern, finally to have it sold from under her by the local hierarchy. Apart from being what she is, Mary has stood for the needs of people and against the pomposity of structures. And that makes less surprising her being with us.

John Hogan has now left the Maryknoll Brothers, after having been ordered out of Guatemala (with the Melvilles) by his order. That is to say, first by the U.S. Government, then by the oligarchy, then by the Guatemalan

Church, finally by his order. Certain chains of command are observed. John left Maryknoll because he saw it as the left hand of economic imperialism—the right being the American military mission there. An old colonialist theme, it seems, missionaries and troops, is now given new flavor under the enlightened American effort. Santayana said, "Those who have not learned the lessons of history are destined to repeat its mistakes." Apparently John has learned, and instead of repeating mistakes, has resolved to mend them in others.

Next is George Mische, who has packed more militancy and service in his thirty-one years than any three activists I know. Married and the father of a two-month-old daughter, George did campus organizing while still in college, labor organizing for the AFL-CIO, plus foreign-aid administration in the Dominican Republic, Honduras, San Salvador, and Guatemala. For four years he worked with delinquents in New York City and New Jersey, two of these years in Harlem. Refreshingly open, resourceful, and resilient, George is one of the few who has earned the label "Christian revolutionary."

There remains Tom Lewis and my brother Dan Berrigan, S.J. It is enough to say of Tom that he has literally put his future on the line by another civil disobedience following our blood-pouring incident at the Baltimore Customs House on October 27. As for my brother, he is no stranger to Church authoritarianism or social injustice. An enormously gifted and prolific writer, he has given meaning to his words by his deeds: working with students among the poor and in behalf of blacks, being exiled to Latin America, jailed in October, and traveling to Hanoi to obtain the release of captured American fliers.

So much for our jail community. Jim Bevel of SCLC once said that the movement ought to fill up the jails of this country. Not to seek jail, mind you, but to practice a level of civil disobedience that would make jail inevitable, the moral complement of activism. Jail and fasting—the movement knows so little about them, and indeed fears them entirely without cause. When movement people other than draft protesters, particulary the clergy, take the spirit of the acts of the Apostles into jail with them, then the movement will have matured, revolution will be less violent, and justice more possible.

A DAY IN THE PEN:
AN INTERVIEW

The following interview was compiled from long Conversations with Phil Berrigan at Union Theological Seminary in May, 1969 and at the Catholic Worker House in Baltimore in June, 1969. The interview is completed at the end of the Journal section.

Q. *You are the first Catholic priest in this country to go to jail as a political prisoner. What does jail mean to you, and what were your first impressions inside a federal penitentiary?*
A. I conceive of jail directly in terms of resistance—that is, how do you embarrass the Establishment, how do you shame them, how do you keep them off balance, how do you continue to bring to light the principles and issues that guide you in a time of grave national crisis? I see jail as an effective part of nonviolent tactics, which really do present alternatives to all sorts of people, and ought to be made policy. The big question, of course, is: How do you refashion this

27

society? How do you bring its power to term, in a human fashion, before it destroys itself?

My very first experience of prison was a week's stay at the Baltimore City Jail after the blood-pouring action in the Baltimore Customs House in October, 1967. There were four of us in that action, two of whom—Jim Mengel and David Eberhardt—were released on their own recognizance; Tom Lewis and I chose to stay in jail for a week and to fast. So we had already had that experience and seen the effect of it, the embarrassment through the penal system—federal officers coming up from Washington, interns waking us up in the middle of the night to check our heart and pulse every four hours because of our fast. When we were jailed the second time, after the Catonsville Nine action, and sent to the Baltimore County Jail, the situation was changed because we had a very, very good warden, a Catholic, and it wasn't as easy to accomplish what we had done the first time—to embarrass the Establishment—because this man was so human, he was so deeply understanding and sympathetic toward what we had done. We stayed in the Baltimore County Jail for about six weeks after Catonsville. We looked forward immensely to getting out of the county jail and being sent to a federal pen, because we had been in a maximum-security cell; and that means that you only leave that cell to eat three times a day, you go down for meals only with your own people from the cell, that's the only activity. At night Tom Lewis and I were in double lockup. With the beautiful weather outside, there was a natural longing to share in it, but this was impossible in the county jail, so we were very happy to be forwarded up to Lewisburg.

The day we left for Lewisburg was a very, very hot July day. We were told about an hour before that we were to be moved, that the federal marshals would be there at such and such a time, to gather our belongings, to get our things

in order. Then we were taken out to the outer office, where
two federal marshals awaited us with their handcuffs and
chains and the necessary transferral papers. The man in
charge was a black guy who was just breaking in on the
job. He apparently had hangups about us at the start—
later, we became very friendly with him—he treated us rather
harshly, abruptly, and he went through the unnecessary
business of putting ankle shackles on us. In addition, we had
to wear a waist chain, and our handcuffs were attached
again to the waist chain, so that we had to hold our hands
in our laps. Then we were brought out to the marshal's car
and put in the back seat. Federal marshals drive their own
cars. The government apparently pays them a mileage rate
for any traveling they do. So the three of us were stuffed
in the back seat, chained together, on a very, very hot day.

Q. *Why three?*
A. A black prisoner was transferred with us. He was facing
two years up at Lewisburg for burglary, I think—Federal
Savings and Loan.

Q. *How long was the trip, Phil?*
A. The trip between Baltimore and Lewisburg, Pennsylvania, would be about three hours. The marshals are obligated to feed you en route if the trip calls for it. So we
stopped at a place beyond Harrisburg just south of the
penitentiary itself. The marshals took our orders: roast-beef
sandwich, cheeseburger, what have you. One of them
zipped into the restaurant and came out with the food, and
of course refused to release our hands at all to help us eat.
You're caught in the position of juggling a hamburger and a
large Coke in hands tied off your waist and shackled together—it's quite a feat. Right after our food was bought, I
think one of us requested to go to the john, and just to give
you an idea of how highly tense the black marshal was, he
drove over to the rear of a gas station, I would say within

ten yards of the john entrance, and very carefully unlocked us. One marshal guarded us while the black guy went to see if anybody was in there. There was, so he waited two or three minutes while the person was finishing up, and then he beckoned to us. So one by one we went to the john, and in the meantime a truck driver, who had stopped for something to eat, also wanted to use this particular john, but the marshal flung out his arms before the entrance and said, "Federal marshal—prisoner inside—will you wait?" Well, the truck driver didn't understand the statement and kept coming, so the black marshal repeated it as an order, "Federal marshal—prisoner inside—wait!" The truck driver was highly embarrassed—first of all, he'd been given an order by a black man, you see; he wasn't used to that. And secondly, there I was—in clerical collar and chains—he had never been in this situation before and was utterly confused, so he lit a cigarette very quickly and kind of gulped it down, and went back to his truck and drove away, without using the facilities.

Q. *Did they take off the ankle shackles or the chain around your waist during this stop?*
A. Yes, we would go in in handcuffs. And we had the great concession of having the handcuffs released from our waist chain, so that we could relieve ourselves.

Q. *The three of you were chained together in the car?*
A. Our ankle shackles were chained together. I was next to the black guy, and Lewis was on my right.

Q. *Could you tell anything about the black guy's reaction? Did you know him in the Baltimore jail?*
A. I had met him at chapel, or worship, one Sunday morning. I think he was a Catholic. He was very well disposed, a Baltimore guy, and knew of our situation, had talked it over with some of the black prisoners there. And he went up

to Lewisburg relieved, kind of, for two reasons. The first was that he was out of Baltimore County Jail, and he'd get to a better situation in a federal pen; that is, better food, more freedom, what have you. And the second thing he was pleased about was that he'd gotten only two years. He expected three or five for what he had done. So he was in a very good frame of mind, and we chatted all the way up there.

Q. *What about the marshals? How would you describe them?*
A. Marshals are not especially formidable-looking, though they have many who are athletic, sturdy, and the burly types. In terms of their job, the custody of prisoners, they don't miss a trick at all. They make an absolutely sure job of moving a guy around, and making sure that he remains in custody. Some are older men pushing fifty who have been in the federal marshal's office for a good twenty-five years, and because of lack of intelligence or initiative, I would suppose, have not risen in their job. Others come from the city and the state police and have been transferred to the federal marshal's office—better security, perhaps a little better pay, work more to their liking. They are very ordinary men, well trained in terms of custodial efficiency. The black marshal was fully six-feet-two, possibly 210 pounds, might have played football in high school or college, handsome, very straight, short-cropped hair, medium dark. Very clipped and abrupt in his speech; short answers, short questions. Would talk to you, though. A large percentage of the marshals are Catholics, and by and large they were so outraged by what we had done that they would call me by my last name, just to convey a point. In their eyes, I had abandoned the values of my priesthood by doing this stupid, rather desperate thing.

Q. *What was the conversation in the car? Was there any conversation between the two guards, or between the three of you, or between any one of the three of you and the guard?*

A. Well, these two particular marshals were new to us, and we had never encountered them before, so our conversation with them, by and large, was light. There was always the possibility of antagonizing the marshals. You hear stories from prisoners from time to time that on these long treks, where a man is being transferred from Atlanta to Lewisburg, to Danbury, to Leavenworth, or some other place, if they are given a particularly bad time, the marshals retaliate in the only way they know. You don't want to provoke that; you keep the conversation light, or you talk about the Orioles; of course, if they want to bring up the question of what you've done, and what you're all about, well, that's fine.

Q. *In that first ride, what did the marshals' conversation consist of?*

A. They would mostly discuss the assignments they had been on, the running around the country they'd done. The black marshal had just transported two women prisoners —very often they are allowed to take their wives along— from Alderson, West Virginia, to the West Coast women's penitentiary, I think, in California, and he was telling about that, and the various problems that arose.

Q. *What were the problems?*

A. The problem of himself and his wife—a black guy and a black woman—transporting two white women and having them in handcuffs, and seeing that supervision was exact on planeboard, and seeing that the women were served; and trying to set up a relationship with these women prisoners. In a paradoxical way, he was interested in them, he wanted to treat them humanly; they were in his care, and he wanted to see that pressures were kept from them in the course of the trip.

Q. *What happened when you got to Lewisburg? What is it like there?*

A. Well, the first view you have of Lewisburg penitentiary . . . It's rather flat Pennsylvania countryside at that point, and as you approach you come to a kind of a brow of a hill, maybe fifty to seventy-five feet above the level of the penitentiary. It's a formidable-looking place built by the WPA labor in the thirties, possibly 1934–35. Reminds you of a kind of medieval city, done in a modern way. All in very substantial red brick, with a huge twenty- or twenty-five-foot wall surrounding the whole enclave.

Then you turn in off the main road, Route 15, and you pass through the guards' community, because all the federal guards live there, if they've been working in the system for long. And you have these marvelous, clean little stereotyped government houses—the clipped lawns, the gardens and flowers, everything immaculate. It reminds you of a military post, such as Fort Bragg, in North Carolina or Fort Benning, in Georgia. Then you go through the lush cornfields, which are associated with the farm compounds outside of the wall where the swine and the dairy cattle are kept. And you approach this huge main gate with a guard overlooking the whole parking area, which is about twenty yards from the main gate. And over the PA system the marshals are asked: "What's your business?" There's a phone at the edge of the parking system, and they communicate with the guard in the upper tower, who is about forty feet up. The marshals say they have a couple of prisoners, and the guard will direct every step of the way from that point on. He'll say: Pull into the parking lot, and stay in the car. Then he'll communicate with Control inside, which is the central control station of the penitentiary, and he'll wait for his instructions, and when he gets them, he'll speak to the marshals again. There again—a very, very hot day, a long trip, ankle shackles—we still weren't allowed out of the car until the guard from the tower told the marshals to bring us out. Then they picked up our belongings—we both had a few books along, and a few extra clothes—released us from ankle shackles, and led us right below the guard's tower. Someone would come down to make an initial check, search us, and then would call someone else from the processing station inside to meet us there. Lewis and I and the black guy, as we were walking to processing, which is kind of on the side of the main building, had to pass along the front of the penitentiary—it happened to be an hour of the afternoon when they had free time and were taking it easy— and all the men in the cells were at the windows looking down on us, a phalanx of faces. The word was spreading fast, and by the time we finally came in contact with the prisoners, literally everyone knew who we were.

Q. *You mean, other war resisters who recognized you?*
A. No, there weren't many resisters there, they'd been sent off to Allenwood. But it should be understood that almost everyone there is anti-federal government—that is, they resist—not so much their conviction or their treatment in court, but their treatment after getting into the federal penal system: the impersonality, the manipulation, the obvious corruption, the hypocrisy, and a lot of other things. You have immediate sympathy, because even though you're there for different reasons than they are, at the same time you're there for the same reasons.

Q. *What do you mean by that?*
A. I don't know if I can make this exactly clear. But the men there, for the most part . . . I won't say all, because a large portion of the prisoners were fat cats who had lived high off the diet of crime and knew precisely what they were doing —some of them highly educated men—they had just chosen beating the system for reasons of security or income, or because they had become addicted to the high life. But the

vast majority of men there were victims of society, men who had never had a chance, either in family background or in institutional life within the society—and a high percentage were blacks. They sensed that somehow this society was not for them; they sensed too that for reasons they could not exactly control, in order to live, and in order to have some hope, the only way was to try to beat the society. Most of them were uneducated people, but they sensed that the whole thing was a mess, that literally almost everybody in America was a thief, and that to get along, and to prosper, and to achieve some sort of identity, you almost *had* to be a thief. And they would tell you astounding tales about the various types of corruption that they had come across, not only in the lower levels of their own communities, but also in the circles of power governing their communities. Some of them were remarkably astute about political corruption in the cities they came from. By and large they were urban types. They sometimes had amazing insights into what the federal government was all about. And they would watch very, very closely within the penal system as to how things were handled, and how some of the ambiguities arose. So we had that common bond with them; in a very wide sense, almost everybody there was a political prisoner. And almost all of them had the firm intention of confronting the system, using the best means at hand, which might very largely mean: Upon release you do what you were doing before. But next time be a bit more smart, and don't get caught.

Q. *Could you describe the processing room at the main penitentiary at Lewisburg? How large was it? Was it a building which was on the outskirts of the jail, or was it central?*

A. It was right near one of the buildings on the outskirts of the jail—that is, on the periphery of the main complex. And it was largely a series of offices. A man would be brought in, a guard would appear. Several inmates were working there; it was a privileged job, incidentally, requiring capable and astute men. You would be told to strip, and all of your clothing would be packed, to be returned to any address you might choose. I had been wearing my clerical clothing, which was the only personal clothing that I had had since entering the Baltimore County Jail. A guard would come along with a flashlight. He would examine your mouth for any deposits that you might want to bring in, and then other orifices. You'd be made to squat. Once the guards were satisfied that you weren't carrying anything, you'd be told to take a shower. There were about four men processing us, and they would immediately strike up conversation. They would ask: Well, where are you from? What are you in for? Then they would be immediately interested, and the conversation would take another tack. They'd tell about the people already there who would be sympathizing with you. They'd tell about the feelings of some of their friends. All of this, of course, would be muttered in an aside so the guards wouldn't overhear. As to the guards, they would restrict their remarks just to business, and it was only after we were there for a while that a guard would begin to inquire more deeply as to what you were about.

After you had showered, you would be given temporary prison clothing and then you would be sent to a rather massive station right in the center of the prison that deals with laundry, new clothing, outfitting, what have you, and there they have perhaps thirty to forty men working, and right adjacent to that area, Jimmy Hoffa was in a separate cage sewing mattresses, so that was our first look at him.

Q. *Did they give you some sort of clothes, or a robe, after the shower?*
A. Yes, they would give you a prison shirt, a kind of blue denim affair, and shorts, pants, and shower sandals.

Q. *Did they let you keep your watch, the medal around your neck?*

A. The watch would have to be turned in, but they would allow you to keep your medal. Also a Bible, one or two books, maybe a few notes you had kept, if they considered them to be harmless. Then you go to the clothing processing, down a hall maybe fifty or sixty yards—it's a very large building, housing twelve hundred men—and right away the prisoners would give you clothing that would fit you, duplicate sizes so you'd have two sets of clothes. They weren't necessarily concerned about the fit, because the uniforms changed at Allenwood. At Lewisburg the men wear blue; at Allenwood they wear suntans, Army suntans.

Q. *Were you and Tom Lewis together at this point?*

A. Tom and I were both at Lewisburg for about three days completing the processing, taking tests, going through a complete physical, but when I was sent to Allenwood, he was sent to the farm outside the wall, as it is called, where the swine are raised and the dairy cattle kept, and the milk produced for the prison system.

Q. *During these three days of processing, what were the doctors like? And there were probably psychiatrists involved, too?*

A. The MDs for the most part there were young Americans who had entered the federal system in order to avoid military service. Despite that fact, they didn't seem especially sympathetic to us. The psychiatrist at the main penitentiary was a West German, let's call him Lukas, who had entered the federal system to avoid military conscription and to assure naturalization. They had offered him a very lucrative bag. He was to serve as head psychiatrist there for three years, and he would gain both of these objectives. But he was a man of too much conscience not to be ashamed of what he had done. And as his sympathy with the antiwar people grew, and as he met more and more of them, and in some cases had them under therapy, he became much more sensitive to his own situation and very honest in admitting his culpability. In fact, he had a good nonviolent orientation, was a very compassionate man, and a damned good psychiatrist as well. Lukas's assistant was a remarkable guy named Roger Stewart, who had gotten something like two and a half years for passing bad checks—a small amount, maybe eight hundred dollars. Stewart was one of the key men in the penitentiary—literally knew everyone, very sensitive guy, maybe thirty-five years old, a civil engineer. He was instrumental in getting both Tom Lewis and me together with Lukas later on. He wanted Tom to work with prisoners in the psychiatric ward, wanted art taught to them, wanted to get them into art as a form of psychiatric therapy. Lukas became a close friend of ours, and recently he and the psychologist at the main penitentiary were two of the key people protesting the procedure of the administration at Lewisburg to send men like Dave Miller—antiwar people— down to the jungle where they would be subject to sexual assault. Both of them said that if this were not corrected immediately they would go to Washington about it.

Q. *What do you mean by the jungle? Were you ever down there?*
A. The jungle was notorious; you'd get all sorts of feedback about it. Generally, new and untried prisoners were sent there, or the old-line prisoners, hard-shell cases, who were interested in pursuing their own interests. Which is to say, they could set up their own kind of intrigues down there, with gambling, narcotics, and homosexual pursuits.

Q. *Why do you say "down there?" Was it actually the lower part of the prison?*
A. Yes, on the same level as processing itself. You could consider it a part of a huge cellar; in effect, it was a huge

dormitory, housing sixty or seventy men in single one-level bunks. The bona-fide homosexual community wasn't there, however; they were kept to themselves and they had an esoteric, isolated community of their own upstairs, because many of them were privileged people who had highly skilled jobs. Many homosexuals were people of unusual background who were in the educational department or were working in the dental laboratory, or with the doctors, or in industry. These men were organic homosexuals and left mostly to themselves. The guys downstairs for the most part were marginal; they would have been heterosexual outside if they had access to women. Anytime a homosexual attack occurred down there, it was mostly brutal in intent rather than homosexual, if that makes any sense. So when the draft resisters would come in there, and many of them had been sent down into the jungle following the kind of holiday unrest at Allenwood, you would have open, friendly, rather well-scrubbed normal types being brought into that kind of environment. And the objective would be to exploit them. And that was largely the reason behind the sexual assaults. There were only a few. There were a lot of threats, but only a few actual assaults.

Q. *From what you say, though, it seems obvious that the prison authorities would be aware of this kind of situation. Why did they tolerate it? Did they tolerate it to intimidate prisoners whom they thought would cause trouble in other areas?*

A. First of all, the objective of the whole administration there is not to have trouble. The good prison administrator, like the man they had there, would be interested in effective means of pacifying people. Not rehabilitation as such, not the service of the men, not their uplift, not their preparation for civilian life later on, but how do you create a static situation while the men are there. So that their job

is easier. By and large this is the rationale. Now, when you
have a dormitory of sixty or seventy men, many of them
violent types, many of them very overt in their hatred of
the administration and of individual guards, an awful lot
can go on: sexual assaults, beatings, threats of all description, organization of cliques and gangs—an awful lot of that
can go on without the administration being aware of it, or
wanting to be aware of it. It's too much for them to handle.
And of course they know enough about the prison mystique
to understand that if things are handled adroitly and really
intelligently, the prisoners will pacify themselves. You just
have to give in here, make an apparent concession here,
you have to throw them a few crumbs here, give them a
few added privileges here, give them more freedom here,
appear to give in to their demands here, see, and they'll
handle themselves. It's divide and conquer, really. And it's
enormously effective. And if push really comes to shove,
and you do have an organized movement against penal
administration—and they realize that this can come at one
time or another—then they know they have the force to put
it down. They have the local and state cops at their command. They can get them in, see, or they can get other
federal marshals in, or they can get the National Guard in;
they know they can put it down.

Q. *How were you brought out of the processing area at
Lewisburg into Allenwood?*
A. Well, there were several buses from Allenwood coming
into Lewisburg every day with people going to the dental
clinic, or to see the doctors, the psychiatrist, if you were
going for release, and so forth. And these buses would usually
go back in the afternoon loaded with people who were being sent to Allenwood. Once you're brought into Allenwood,
you face an orienting officer, and he will take you through
an explanation of about three hours of what you are allowed

to do there; what your duties will be; what mealtimes are; when the clinics run—all of these things. And he'll spend a great deal of time telling you where you are *not* to walk, where you are to walk, and how much freedom you have....

Q. *Were you alone with the officer when he told you this?*
A. There was a group of about fifteen of us being briefed together. Some of them were antiwar people, including a couple of Jehovah's Witnesses, and the rest of the group was filled out by ordinary prisoners of various types.

Q. *And what was the chap like who briefed you?*
A. He was a man about fifty-five years old who had been through World War II and had entered the federal service after that, and had been a guard at various federal penitentiaries around the country. He had been out in the Midwest to one or two places. He had already been to Danbury, and now he was a guard at Allenwood. He was a man who was kind of hard-bitten, not too bright, interested mostly in the mailed fist, who would tell you very concretely and very harshly what you could do and what you couldn't do. He would conclude by saying, "There's a pretty livable life here, if you behave, and if you don't, you're going to get your ass in a sling. And you're going to be called in the office here, and you're going to be sent back to the main penitentiary." The main penitentiary at Lewisburg was a threat they would constantly hold over you. Because it was a maximum-security place, all walled in except for the farm outside the walls, where Tom Lewis was sent. So Allenwood was looked upon as a privilege. There were easier work conditions at Allenwood, and fewer restrictions of freedom. And also, if you were sent back to Lewisburg you might have to go through a version of court again—that is, you would have to deal with some of the associate wardens, who would have all the available evidence at hand and would charge

you and convict you. And the conviction could very well be isolation for a time, or the hole, or possibly even a threat that you be transferred to another penitentiary around the country.

Q. *What happened after the briefing?*
A. It was late in the afternoon. First of all, we had a late lunch, and then we went to pick up our clothing, which means we had to turn in all of the blue clothing we had, and pick up the suntans. They were used, but they were very, very clean, immaculately clean. A great laundry service there. And then you'd be assigned a bunk. When new people would arrive at Allenwood—which was, incidentally, an ordnance ammunition depot in World War II, converted by the federal government into a penal reservation—they'd be sent to a building where people would be sleeping double tier, one above the other. The building was in extremely decrepit shape. It was not at all uncommon to see mice at night. It had already been condemned repeatedly by the federal government as a fire hazard, and ought to have been torn down as unsafe. At the time I was there we had possibly 135 men in this building; safely, I suppose, it should have accommodated perhaps forty or fifty at the most. The shower and washroom facilities for 135 men were of course largely inadequate. Anyway, the new arrivals would be fitted into that system, and according to your longevity at the reservation, you would be moved slowly into newer dormitories, which in turn would accommodate about one hundred apiece. So the thing to do was to put in a cop-out as soon as you came to Allenwood, in order to get better quarters later on, and then the list would be taken in series.

Q. *What do you mean by cop-out?*
A. A cop-out is a form that is filled out and turned in to administration regarding any requests whatsoever: for a

new job, for better quarters, for an interview with the social worker—anything like that.

Q. *What was a typical day at Allenwood like? At what time would you wake up?*
A. The first buzzer would go off at six-thirty. And some men would immediately get up, go and get shaved, and very quickly get cleaned up and go to breakfast. Some would not eat breakfast; they would sleep until seven-thirty. That's optional, if you want to do it. Others would kind of straggle out between seven and seven-thirty. I hadn't been there more than two weeks before the chaplain over at the main penitentiary got me permission to say a private mass down at the chapel, which was on the lower end of the reservation, about a mile away. It was an old Protestant church that was used for both Protestant and Catholic services. So I used to run down there: get up at six-thirty and trot down there, say a very quick mass, and then come back for breakfast. When I first started, I'd go down every morning, and then I found this kind of burdensome. I felt very, very deeply, too, the fact that nobody was allowed to worship with me. Later on, I'd go about every other day. And on Sundays I'd worship with the prisoners.

Q. *And then you'd go to breakfast. What was that like?*
A. You would go through a cafeteria line. And the food, in terms of substance and nutrition, was always superb. Many of their own vegetables were grown right in the area; you'd get fresh vegetables and tomatoes during the summer. The meat, even though it was only served once a day and in limited quantities, would be excellent: fine pork and beef, and in some cases even steak, since they were raising their own cattle. You would have some milk, there would be fruit juice. And of course the prisoners did the baking, and the baked goods would be excellent. The bread was almost Trappist-like in its quality and content,

and of all descriptions: white bread, whole wheat, rye, and really superior buns from time to time for breakfast. Twice a week you would get eggs, and their own home-grown bacon. At other times you would have a pick of good dry cereal, or substantial oatmeal. So the food, by and large, I would say, was excellent. There would be a lot of crabbing about it, because some rather esoteric tastes weren't being served, but I thought it was great.

Q. *Did you eat at long tables? How many people would each table hold?*
A. No, you'd have a little circular table accommodating four men. It's a fine institution, because it gives you an opportunity to get to know almost everybody.

Q. *Any restrictions on talking?*
A. No restrictions on talking whatsoever. And a man who was really interested in meeting everyone and creating friendships can just rotate every meal, and meet new people every meal. There was a high degree of clique atmosphere there, some people always sitting with one another. But if you were really interested, you could get to know the whole prison population in the space of two to three months, just by doing a little thinking, and by going to their tables.

Q. *Did you do that? Did you try to rotate and meet new people all the time?*
A. Yes, I did, except that I was working with the antiwar people and of course the main burden of my business was with them. Some of them weren't on the farm crew, and the only opportunity I had to see them was during meals, so I kind of looked for them. But when that opportunity didn't present itself, then I looked for the blacks, and the Jewish community, and the Mafia people.

Q. *What about Hoffa?*
A. I heard more about Hoffa than I actually heard from him

directly. Hoffa is a kind of political prisoner and was going through severe harassment at Lewisburg, and was making his own response to it, which was not beyond his resources, because he is a very tough and resourceful man, a man who had been through all kinds of political wars and knew in a very real and experiential sense what the exercise of power in American society was about. My contact with him came one evening when I was out during recreation period at the main penitentiary before transport to Allenwood; a couple of friends of his, who had just happened to hear of the case of Tom Lewis and me and the other people from Catonsville, offered to bring him over. For the most part, Hoffa was extremely circumspect about associations with prisoners; he was a man who would operate only with those he trusted. He was not one to approach the larger community there, and did not speak with everyone. Anyway, he came over that evening, and there were a lot of implications operating in his attitude toward me. Number one was that we were political prisoners together. Number two was that I was a priest—don't forget, Hoffa came out of the Catholic tradition, and was of course an ethnic-group Catholic. He was not prepared to see a priest in jail. So without listening to me much, he announced that he understood a lot of the crap from the prison authorities under which I would be operating, and that he had resources at his command to help me with this kind of pressure. He foresaw for me, in effect, the same kind of oppression that had afflicted him ever since he had been at Lewisburg. And he said, you know our people are over at Allenwood, and our people are at the farm outside the wall, and we have our people here. If there's anything that you need, you merely inform this one or that one. And word will be gotten back to me, and we'll see that you get it. In addition, he said, if you're harassed or if you're oppressed, or if you're treated contemptibly, or if you're given the wrong kind of job, we want to know about it immediately, and we'll take measures to straighten it out. So I thanked him, and we had a very warm handshake, and I went about my business and he went about his.

My contact with Jimmy Hoffa after that meeting was mostly through the people who were working with him, and they comprised roughly two groups, or two communities, both at Lewisburg, the farm outside the wall, and also at Allenwood. The first community was made up of the people from the Teamsters Union who were in jail with Hoffa. There was one guy in particular, the local business agent for the largest Teamsters local in the country, who was in jail at that time in Allenwood, and of course a very dear and devoted friend of Jimmy's. There were other Teamster officials there, and closely aligned with them would be the people from the Pennsylvania miners' unions: John L. Lewis' United Mine Workers, now headed of course by Boyle. The second group that would be intensely involved with Jimmy would be either marginal or substantial Mafia people from the New Jersey or Metropolitan areas of New York— the Italian ethnic-group community. At Allenwood you had representatives of all these special-interest groups, and I maintained a very good relationship with them. They were sympathetic to me; they came from largely Catholic backgrounds. There was the political aspect, there was also the common Catholic background, and there was the fact that I was kind of approachable and human, I suppose, and would listen to them. And so the feedback to Hoffa was rather constant. And from time to time representatives from Allenwood would go to see Jimmy and would confer with him. They were able to manage this because they could put themselves on sick call, or they could go over for a dental appointment, and in the course of being there for the whole morning over at Lewisburg main penitentiary, they could engineer a meeting with Jimmy, and they could bring him up to date on things, and he in turn would keep them informed. So there was this kind of communications network that had been erected long ago and was still in the process of operation.

Q. *What kind of work were you assigned at Allenwood?*
A. I was given an option between the farm and the mess hall, so I said, I'll work in the mess hall here for a while, cleaning up the tables, and resetting the refectory after meals, cleaning up the floor. They kept it in very, very good shape. It was a limited facility, but they made it serve as well as they could.

The superintendent was a Catholic, a World War II veteran. He was a southern Ohio man, a kind of hinterlands type, of the kind so common in the Midwest. He was intrigued not only by the number of Catholics who were involved in antiwar activity but also by the first priest there. We had some good conversations. He was a man, for example, who was disturbed about all the changes in the Church. He didn't understand them—which perhaps gives an insight into how much he was disturbed by men willing to come to jail because of conscience. It was an entirely new phenomenon for him. He was a rather robust man, quite sincere, only rather limited. So we discussed job possibilities back and forth, and we finally decided that I would work in the mess hall. And I did. It was a very nice job, because you'd work only during and shortly after meals, and you'd have a couple of hours off until the next meal, and then you'd have the afternoon off until the evening meal; and after you'd cleaned up in the evening, you had most of the evening off. In addition, through rotation and because they had so many people there they couldn't find jobs for, you would have a couple of days off a week. Since I intended to do a lot of reading and writing, and get to work with the antiwar people, all this was very satisfactory.

Well, after working in the mess hall for a couple of weeks,

I saw the need for some exercise, and I also felt keenly about being separated from most of the antiwar people, who were out on the farm, so I transferred to the farmwork. That involves a variety of jobs: you build fences, you repair fences, you clean up the cattle guards—they are a series of iron rails welded together and placed in the middle of the road so the cattle cannot cross. The cattle guards become filled up with dung, dirt, and rain wash, and they have to be lifted up and cleaned out—it's a rather tedious job. On the farm you're doing that, or cutting fence posts, or cleaning out the barns. After working at a variety of tasks for about two weeks, I got on to the manure detail, and about four of us were cleaning out barns. Because they didn't have adequate labor in the past, the barns had filled up with manure. They have to winter some of the cattle inside in order to get them ready for market. That means that the manure just builds up and up, and some of these barns would have an accretion of two or three feet of manure. It would be so compressed and so degenerated and so rich that you would have to peel it off in tiny layers, a couple of inches at a time.

Q. *That's the best kind of manure.*
A. Oh, marvelous stuff. And we'd load it into a manure spreader, and then the tractor would tow it out and put it on the fields. They'd be back in half an hour, and we'd throw another load in. I remember one barn in particular where we worked almost three weeks to clean it out.

Q. *Who were you working with?*
A. I was working with a couple of antiwar people, and then later, with a bootlegger from Virginia who used to make this marvelous applejack. He used to explain the formula for it over and over again. Real lovely guy. In addition, he drove his own tractor trailer along the interstate bit, and would haul anything. He even had his tractor trailer paid for. Ap-

parently he'd make an awful lot of applejack, sell some of it, make a little profit on it, drink a lot of it himself. Marvelous guy.

Q. *How many years did he get for bootlegging?*
A. One, but with his good time he'd probably not serve more than about eight months. And he wasn't a standard server. He was taking it very, very coolly. His home situation was intact; you know, his wife was a good woman, he had a couple of teen-agers, and the kids were doing all right. So he took it very placidly, the whole thing.

Q. *At what time did you finish work?*
A. We would return from work back to the main compound at three-thirty or a quarter to four, and we'd have to stand head count at four o'clock. The count itself was extremely important on the reservation there; the officials took it very seriously. If a man wasn't where he was supposed to be, and if he didn't appear at the various counts during the day and night—there were six of them, all told—then there would be all sorts of shuffling around; either they'd produce the body or they'd call people in from outside, and they'd begin to scour the roads around the camp. While I was there, per-haps two men escaped, and they were very quickly picked up because they apparently left under the stress of emotion and without a plan, and were noticed in nearby towns. At any rate, we'd go to supper after head count, and supper was again a kind of community thing. You'd always be able to sit down with people you wanted to see and to talk to, and then it would be a rare opportunity to talk with new people, with whom a lot of us thought it important to es-tablish a relationship. After supper, let's say six o'clock, I used to steal away for two or three hours and get down to the education department to do some solid reading and writing, until the evening count, which was at nine sharp.

Q. *What kind of reading and writing? Could you read anything there, and what kind of writing did you do? Was this mostly letters, or was it more a philosophical thinking-through of issues and so forth?*

A. It was mainly the type of political writing, from a Christian standpoint, that I had been doing before, and my reading was the best I could pick up in a tiny little library of about five hundred volumes that they had, which was reinforced by books that were circulating among the antiwar people and the more political people around Allenwood, and also a fair range of periodicals that were coming in to the political people or to the library itself. I remember reading *The Robber Barons,* for example—that was a great favorite there. *Containment and Change* was around. There was a very detailed government study that the library got its hands on as to the effects of not only Hiroshima but also the nuclear testing around Bikini and the Pacific. The librarian gave that to me, and there were several volumes by Martin Buber that I read. And they'd have a daily paper down there; we used to get the *Philadelphia Inquirer,* and also the *Washington Post,* one day late. Many people had subscribed to *The New York Times,* and I finally got on some sort of waiting list for that; I'd get it about two days late and would go through it thoroughly. So there were many items of current news to pick up, and one had a chance to reflect on their wider meaning.

Q. *Did you ever see* The Wall Street Journal *while you were there?*

A. No, I didn't know anyone who was getting *The Wall Street Journal,* though it might well be, since they had a lot of Establishment people from the metropolitan area there. Anyway, by and large, the literary climate wasn't too bad if one worked at it. I'd be reading down there and was also working on a manuscript. Of course, since I had been for-

bidden about half a dozen times to disobey the prison regulations regarding writing, I was very circumspect about it
and used to rotate from scene to scene and from night to
night. I'd do a little writing in about three different spots:
up in the dormitories, down in the education department,
or, as long as the light lasted, sometimes I would go out
and work outside.

The regulations could be gotten around, particularly if
a language was worked out. Some of the prisoners, of course,
had a rather detailed and ingenious code worked out with
their immediate friends or family. Soon after I got there
the head clerk in administration—I got friendly with him—
told me that an order had come from the superintendent's
office to keep a close eye on all the typewriters in the institution, and that I was not to be allowed near them. It
was sort of a silly order, but apparently they were extremely
apprehensive about my writing. Of course, they knew that
I did write from time to time. The Superintendent called
me in twice to read me the federal regulations against political writing, and every time I saw him after that he would
remind me of my responsibilities in this regard. And he
would reemphasize that they didn't care about my writing,
but what I wrote had to be sent to Washington for censorship. If you wanted to do a philosophical piece, or if you
wanted to write sociology, or if you wrote on theology or
anything like that, it would probably pass through rather
easily in Washington, but if you wanted to do political
writing, and above all if you wanted to do anything on the
penal system, then of course it was useless to try. You could
talk to prisoners who had tried, particularly some of the old-
liners over at Lewisburg. All sorts of ingenious ways have
already been perfected by prisoners to get material out. One
guy, for example—as the visitors drove out, as they headed
for Route 15, which is about a mile away past a country
club, they'd stop at a set point in the road as they ap-

proached Route 15, and there was a large boulder there, and they'd pick up the boulder and he'd have something underneath for them.

Q. *Was there any opportunity in the evenings for people to get together for common recreation, and was that time available for any kind of group discussion or study? Or was that reserved just for weekends or for time off when you wouldn't normally be working?*

A. No, there was a great deal of that going on in the evening. Soon after I arrived there, through the acquaintances I had with the antiwar people especially, and also with a larger representation within the community, it became very apparent to me that there wasn't much moral and intellectual formation going on there, and that there was really a lot of fragmentation within the draft-resister community. So we talked a great deal about it, and finally agreed to meet. The draft resisters there had already gone through a couple of abortive attempts to sustain themselves in some sort of loose community and to meet regularly, and I think twice previously they had gotten permission for this, but it had folded. The Catholic chaplain wasn't open to this sort of thing; it was useless to approach him. We got permission for meetings through the Protestant chaplain, who was a very fine man. He was no radical, in any sense of the word, but he worked very hard at counseling, at providing better literature for the men, at keeping up more human relationships, and doing what he could with the very inbred and stolid administration over at the main penitentiary.

So, along with some of the Catholic Worker people that I knew well, we started in, and slowly the group built up to about fifteen men. Some weeks we would have as many as two meetings, rather long and sustained sessions that would run perhaps three hours. This was really quite a feat, and perhaps it indicates the level of interest that was being

mobilized. Because these guys would come in very tired
from the farm, kind of exhausted, and yet would stick
around in a broiling room in one of the dormitories for a
meeting that would run that long. Our view was, by and
large, that the community ought to be an inclusive one,
because it ought to be reaching out to the other communities
in the prison—the Jewish community, the veterans' bunch
that was around, the Italian ethnic group (including the
Mafia), the black community, and then the poor white community, mostly from the Appalachian area. We ought to be
reaching all of them; that was one concern. In addition, we
ought to be preparing ourselves for the time when we would
be released from jail, so that we could be of use to the
country and mankind. We tried to organize the meetings
along those lines: how we could better serve the Allenwood
community, in addition to that, how we could better prepare
ourselves for life after jail. The penal system was an objective and a concern for resistance but not, I would say, a
primary one.

Q. *Were you able to work with any kind of program, or was
the thing spontaneous from meeting to meeting? Did
you have any kind of text to work with?*
A. Well, it became very programmed after about four or
·five meetings. We wanted to get into the education department, because here we could have a greater impact on the
prison community. It was also important to establish lines
of communication with people outside, particularly those
supporting us. We knew that we needed a better level not
only of discussion but also reading, and, above all, to be
more human and more open. The pressures under which
some of the young guys were operating were extreme, and
were reflected in all sorts of ways. But these meetings, the
discussion of common concerns, had a very definite therapeutic value. You could see men's spirits begin to pick up;

they realized that they weren't alone and isolated; now they had a means for tapping into this other guy who would have his own contribution and would give his support and even stand with them.

Q. *You talk about community concerns and personal problems; how did these questions relate to the more political level of discussions? Was it on the basis of individual witness, or was it more a group-therapy type of situation related to both personal concerns and public issues?*

A. Rather, it was highly politicized. I would say that the majority of the guys there adopted a highly secularistic view, not only of what they had done, but of what they were doing then and what they would do later on. We didn't overtly or directly face up to moral issues. Even with the Catholics there—the Catholic Worker people and the others who came from Catholic colleges and from the Resistance—we didn't suggest, for example, that we ought to take up sustained study of the Scriptures, or anything like that. It was more or less accepted as a general theme that morality was resident in this community and that its members stood for deeply central moral concerns, and that there was a relationship between these concerns and their political objectives. The therapeutic value of these encounters was indirect and came largely from the fact that the young guys understood that friendships were building up, that a community of sorts was being established, and that they not only were being better armed to face the stresses of prison but also were being enlightened as to what they should do once they left Allenwood.

Q. *Did people outside the Resistance involve themselves in these meetings and discussions, and did they stick with it? The contacts and friendships with non-Resistance types—did these things happen outside of the group?*

A. There was one remarkable man who initially began to work with the group simply because I asked him. He was completely acceptable to the draft resisters because he had done a lot of work with them, in terms of friendship, discussion, even counseling, before I arrived. He was extremely close to a nucleus of about twelve. And when the proposal was broached that he come into it, and that he outline proposals and provisions, and even chair the meetings, this was completely acceptable. However, there was another man who tried to break into it, a journalist. By and large, however, because of personal difficulties, he was unacceptable. After I left Allenwood, I am told, he did come into the group; he was very eager to do so.

Q. *Did these people see resistance as a personal thing, or more as a challenge to the conscience of the community?*
A. You have to understand that people had gone into resistance for a vast variety of both personal and public reasons. There was a Jehovah's Witnesses community there, for example. They were more or less exclusive, in the sense that three times a week, a minimum, they would meet by themselves for prayer, for discussion, for group reading, and a variety of other activities that were part of their *modus operandi* there. They even took their recreation mostly together. They weren't approached, because it was known that they wouldn't respond. This is not to denigrate them; they simply were not political people. Of course, as a kind of thematic pattern for their lives, they were anti-government, whatever the government might be. They ran into all sorts of ambiguities along these lines. For example, many of them would work very, very hard supporting the federal operation there; many of them were extremely skilled farmers and were accustomed to a lot of hard work from their early years, and would kill themselves on the farm.

But with the conventional resisters, you would run into a guy—I remember one from Long Island—who wasn't interested in anything but returning to normalcy, as he viewed it; he just didn't want to be involved in killing. He resented very much the idea of military control of him while in service, and paid the price of rejecting it, but he had no politics at all. Even though he was an ex-Catholic, he had a great deal of trouble associating his stand with the traditional moral expression of the Church, or with some of its more progressive voices, or with the directives of Vatican II. He was just sweating it out. He would come around very conscientiously, and he'd try to keep himself open, but he had a great deal of difficulty understanding what the rest of us were about, and why we would want to sustain the resistance we began in the first place.

And there would be others who would say, well, jail is a completely useless process. We want to experience it and understand it, since we are here, but after that we would take measures to get out, meaning anything from accepting parole into the Army to full cooperation with the system in order to get a quick parole, a conventional parole.

In addition, there were some who were being radicalized more and more all the time. I remember one Harvard student, a very remarkable young man who had worked in the McCarthy campaign in a sustained fashion all through the summer of 1968 in the New England area, and had done it at great sacrifice to himself. He needed to earn money, and yet he felt himself compelled to pursue this political tack. But he saw the failure of everything that McCarthy stood for, and he felt that American politics as they had become institutionalized had no room at all for a man like Gene McCarthy, and that he could not be successful. This student's exposure at Allenwood corroborated his view, and he became more radicalized and even revolutionary while he was there, and I am sure is pursuing the same direction now, content with the role he was pursuing in jail and seeing a value in it. So, there were all sorts of viewpoints operating as to why people had come to Allenwood, what they should do while they were there, and what they ought to prepare themselves for later on.

You asked before about the way the day ended. At nine o'clock there was a count, and then we had an hour until ten, when lights went out. People were allowed to stay up until eleven, so during the hot weather there'd be a lot of conversation outside, bull-session stuff, some of it very good. And then people would go to bed at eleven. During the course of the night you were counted three times—a little after midnight, then I think at two-thirty, and then at four-thirty. The guards would come around and take an extremely precise count. They had it all memorized where everyone was supposed to be, and didn't wake anybody up. Everyone got up at six-thirty. Anyway, that gives you, more or less, the framework of the day.

PRISON JOURNAL, 1968

July 11

Although it would be wrong to describe the United States as a police state, it is safe to say that political writing (from any ideology) is a dangerous adventure in federal prison. Second only to escape. Obviously, my presence here indicates the threat I constitute outside—a threat both vocal and physical, flowing directly from my convictions. My "rehabilitation" would mean a reformation. And the way to promote this, apparently, is a heavy prison sentence plus suppression of free expression. In a word, I no longer possess the rights accorded "free" citizens.

Therefore, when opportunities arise, I must circulate through the Allenwood camp area to carefully selected spots —the rec hall one day, writing cubicles in dormitories another, an isolated spot on the grounds a third. And I must be suspicious not only of the guards, but of certain inmates as well, who commonly act as camp intelligence to gain privileges or shortened sentences. My pretext? Writing letters, reading, or simulating a homesick daydream.

A strenuous form of censorship, to be sure, but to a priest who has struggled through the doldrums of Church censorship, merely a restriction of degree, and a challenge to conviction and ingenuity.

The official Church has lost its fight to maintain control of thought; it must now rely on the indirect repression employed by other bureaucracies that control their subjects by institutionalizing self-interest. In a capitalist society, whose very survival depends on its proving that self-interest can be profitable and socially manageable, human freedom undergoes a redefinition, becoming subject to the profit motive which informs society. In this context, freedom is tolerated, encouraged, even made marketable—except when it interferes with production and sales. In effect, freedom is no more than freedom to pursue self-interest within rigidly defined lines, so that the conflicts that emerge might be socially harmonized.

But one looks in vain for a minimally enlightened self-interest on the part of church and government. It would appear that the mark of a mature society is the concern it manifests for people. But when church and government achieve a détente by playing only a slight variation of theme on the old saw of power, one becomes a spectator of social dissolution. The cry of "revolution" begins to be heard more frequently and more urgently.

July 12

Several months of jail have stimulated reflection on the quality of rehabilitation offered by the prison system. Rehabilitation is a large question, and the more one considers it, a despairing one. What, one might ask, is the inmate being rehabilitated for? Is it for middle-class solvency and therefore for tax-paying to finance abominable welfare systems and massive war expenditures? Is it for a solid and righteous stance supporting national racism? Is it for residence in a cultural desert whose values are as violent as they are sterile? Is it for church membership when the Church is little more than an ethical patron to the champions of raw power? Sincere prison officials apparently conceive of rehabilitation as realizing all these goals. Paradoxically, however, rehabilitation is not being realized—even for these targets.

An income-tax evader—one of many here—talked to me recently of his case. A professional man and a Catholic in high standing, he had defrauded the government in 1963. Given a short sentence after offering to make restitution, he mops a corridor for a half-hour each morning, devoting the remainder of the day to socializing and idleness. In his case, as in that of the majority, incarceration is simply punitive. Jail is an attempt to convince both him and his immediate circle that the rules of the game must be kept. And that's rehabilitation.

Another inmate—a bank robber ("Why knock people in the head when there's banks around?")—put it this way: "If a guy decides to rehabilitate himself, he gets rehabilitated. But there's no help doing it. You're like an alcoholic with no AA around." Everyone, in a word, gets the point that the rules must be kept, but there's no help to be had in keeping them outside. And above all, there's no help for those trying to go beyond the rules of enlightened self-interest toward a more basic and human style of life.

Again: Why? Because ours is a waste society. It would seem that as long as human and material waste is kept within tolerable bounds it will remain so; we begin by exploiting the riches of nature for profit and end by exploiting people for the same reason. Our nearly uninhabitable cities, our commercialized and ravaged countrysides, our polluted water and dirty air only parallel human casualties;—all of us are prisoners, even if only a tiny fraction of us are behind bars. Indeed, environmental and human waste is so profound that we cannot duck the overarching questions: Can mere rules-keeping preserve a viable society? If so, what percentage of its citizens must keep the rules to preserve its viability; and does the waste present even in the lives of the rules-keepers suggest the need for measures more strenuous than reform?

In a word, rehabilitation is educational—in the jargon of social science—punitively rather than programmatically. Even if it were programmatically superior—operating on the premise that it is desirable to return men to society *on society's* terms—it would still be a moral and political failure. Our society controls its casualties very well through its prisons, mental institutions, military conscription, and technological patronage.

July 14

I lost my temper and raged inexcusably at a poor lad who was unceremoniously dumped at our cellblock a week ago. He seemed hopeless. Why, he told us later; a conviction for manslaughter, a sentence heavy for one so young; privileges defaulted for jumping a work-release program. The boy's world had fallen to pieces; he could neither understand nor deal with the scraps left him.

One night soon after his arrival he began to chatter convulsively, then suddenly broke down and cried, like a small and helpless boy. We watched him amazed. Was he resilient, or unstable, or both? Presently, judging me more willing than the others to listen, he chose me for his captive audience. He told me he had a brother in Viet Nam, a paratrooper, and how proud he was of him. "Sure like to be there with him," he said. "Better than being here in jail!"

"Why is it better?" I asked, thinking simplemindedly of different kinds of captivity.

"More excitement," he answered. "Feel more like a man getting one of them little mothers in your sights."

I remarked that there was no chance of his going to Viet Nam. Even if he had served his sentence, there was still his record. But out of sheer curiosity I asked, "What if you were free, what's your real reason for wanting to go?"

"Because you gotta," he retorted. "It's your duty!"

"But what if you think the war is wrong?"

"Right or wrong, you owe it to the country. Somebody's got to stop them commies. If I had my way, we'd walk in there and clean 'em out!"

That was enough for me. As I saw it, he was playing games with both his own life and the lives of others. The old gorge rose, and I tore into him, quite happy in my self-righteousness. I told him he was a barbarian for talking that way, that there were only losers in total or nuclear war. How would he feel if the bomb were dropped on him and other Americans?

He sat stunned and unbelieving, not knowing what to say.

I pressed my unfair advantage with relish. I pointed out to my woeful friend that what he was saying was exactly what those most responsible for the war wanted him to say; that they would feed him into the war hopper right away, except for his record. I asked him to tell me what was the difference between him and the Hitler Youth, whose bones were now scattered over Europe. And I wound up my eloquent remarks with a few sharp words on conscience: that a man is a man when his conscience and his life are consistent, and that he had better die than damage his conscience in a serious matter.

He said not another word, nor did he speak the next day. Later, it became clear that he thought me just another adult provost who had ganged up on him. In a sense, he was right. His experience had been such that he could neither understand nor respond to what I said. If anything, my words had deepened his sense of uncertainty and helplessness. Several times, up to the day he was taken away and brought to a state prison farm, I heard him sobbing at night in his cell next door and calling incoherently for help.

What I did was inexcusable, but what had angered me was not the boy but the society or the system that had victimized and exploited him. It is not enough to play the good social scientist and cite the conventional sources of exploitation: divorced parents and chaotic family life, if any; religiosity rather than religion; education of a commonly sterile kind; mechanical surrogates—an obsession with drag racing and high-compression engines; peer-group corruption—running with a group older and equally aimless. The roots of that young and tortured life were in such toxic soil.

The murder of Robert Kennedy set off a frantic debate about violence which clarified little beyond one fact—the guilt of Americans regarding it. Commentators generally said nothing about guilt, but most of them agreed that Americans are a violent people, citing as evidence everything from FBI reports to the Viet Nam war. Which is to leave the issue of violence in midair, simply because we are no more violent than any other people. But our attachments are more violent. And to tell people that they watch too much violence on TV, or own too many guns, or buy their kids too many war toys is to deal only superficially with the problem of attachments. Rather, they must be told why mayhem on TV is so compulsively popular, why they are so fearful that they arm themselves, why war games for kids are small-scale apings of adult violence. But such talk undercuts both the system and its values, because such talk is more than reformist; it is revolutionary.

Yet the longer we put off telling the truth, the more will our delay punish us. Voluntarily or involuntarily, Americans must accept the fact that poverty, racism, and war are the problems of the rich before they are the problems of the poor, the blacks, and the Vietnamese. But today we insist on looking at poverty, racism, and war the other way around; we say that the poor, the blacks, and the Vietnamese are the problems. And that solves nothing; in effect, it only worsens the real problem.

Otherwise intelligent people often speculate uneasily about the obsolescence of national institutions and deplore institutional stagnancy and imperviousness to change. The fact, however, is exactly the contrary. Institutions take their lead from the economic bureaucracy, which is acutely sensitive to change, and changes rapidly—but only in the direction of vested interest and under the heading of survival and expansion. In this sense, institutionalized power is obsolescent. The assumption on which it operates—that everyone benefits from a constantly expanding economy—is totally unsupported by evidence. Against this bureaucratic power stands what is loosely called "the movement," which holds that change ought to benefit those who most need it. Only out of the conflict between these two ideas will come the kind of change that justice requires. But the efforts to shape a better future for our country will, alas, probably involve tumult and upheaval.

The casualties of our society fill this jail, as they fill all the areas of the world that are threatened by our investments and arms. For the Christian, perhaps, the best hope lies in becoming another social casualty, but of a different kind. By exposing himself freely to the punishments society inflicts on its victims, he can give meaning to their powerlessness. Which is to say that a "Great Society" worthy of the name may take the strongest of its infant breaths in jail.

July 24

To build up a life in prison that might have some useful-
ness is a formidable task and a painfully slow one. First of
all, one must relate to a large group of strangers, who can
duplicate neither the sophisticated generosity of my friends
in the peace movement nor the devotion of the blacks in my
parish. Secondly, Big Brother (the administration) keeps
me under steady surveillance. They realize as keenly as I do
the significance of my presence here, and they view that
presence primarily in terms of threat.

One of the clerks told me that prior to my arrival he
received orders to keep the office typewriters covered or
under watch that no one should allow me near one. Today
the superintendent asked me bluntly if I had been writing
articles since my arrival, and asserted that nothing—absolutely nothing—could be said about the life here. When I inquired if regulations permitted political writing, he answered
that such material would have to be reviewed in Washington.

This is another example of the logic of bureaucracy—it
refuses to permit forces under its control to undercut it. I
have embarrassed it twice, maybe even hurt it, and its fear
is shown by a consistent overestimation of my influence and
following.

I must allay their fears, when the opportunity arises, by
telling them that this place is the poorest of targets. This
prison, like Harlem or Viet Nam, has no priority for change
simply because it is no more than an effect to a cause—no
more than a manifestation of a unique form of spiritual
malaise, reinforcing itself by the social mechanisms it
creates. Freeing the spirit would mean destroying those
mechanisms that stupefy, falsely reward, and brutalize it,
both as institution and as penal system.

Perhaps the most important contribution to be made to

this effort is to study the machines that power uses to maintain itself—for such study will reveal where its vulnerability lies. In the present context, truth is an embarrassment and justice is a threat. Any attack on the present operation of power, any call for an exposure, only forces the guardians of the system to react. We should keep in mind that the system is corrupt enough to be both absurdly inept and surprisingly vulnerable, remaining at the same time devious, subtle, flexible before threats, and immensely powerful. It is not an adversary for the confused, the fatalistic, or the fainthearted.

A deeply respected friend who is also a priest told me that he had seriously considered going to Viet Nam to bear arms with the National Liberation Front. He has learned better since! The real target is here at home.

July 25

Yesterday I returned from eight days away, most of it spent in Baltimore for discussion with lawyers of our fall trial. A court writ was delivered here; Tom Lewis and I were moved to Lewisburg for processing; the discharge department dressed us carefully in civilian clothes, handcuffed us to federal marshals, and off we went. No one had consulted us about our desires, and we had only a vague idea of our destination and its purpose. In common with prisoners everywhere, we were very nearly at the complete disposal of the law. There is nothing to sustain a man except the need to continue, and in my own case, confidence in my integrity.

Two days were spent traveling and going through the interminable red tape connected with leaving prison and returning to it. Talking to our lawyers and friends took a few hours. The remaining time was spent waiting for return here. It is an experience closely related to being nowhere—one is neither where one belongs nor at the pitiful base of operations inflicted by conviction for "crime."

It would be nonsense to pretend that we feel no sense of mission, no sense that we have served God and man by choosing a consequence in general second only to death. That is why it seems terrible to be so compromised by being placed in this vacuum between stations, which is especially destructive to a sense of purpose. One learns patience, however, and tries to hand more and more over to God for his disposal, while continuing to expand one's human interests and responsibility. All of which requires that one accept the Lord as Lord, while proving oneself the Lord's friend and brother. ". . . I call you not servants . . . but I have called you friends. . . ." John 15:15.

July 26

I have been reading Ignazio Silone's *Bread and Wine* with great relish and greater gratitude. Silone expands his view of freedom through Pietro Spina, an Italian revolutionary who is his "majority of one during Italy's absurd Ethiopian war."

Spina says, "Liberty isn't a thing you are given as a present. You can be a free man under a dictatorship. It is sufficient if you struggle against it. He who thinks with his own head is a free man. He who struggles for what he believes to be right is a free man. Even if you live in the freest country in the world and are lazy, callous, apathetic, irresolute, you are not free, but a slave, though there be no coercion and no oppression. Liberty is something you have to take for yourself. It is no good begging it from others."

It may seem surprising to some that my freedom here is more full and satisfying than any previously experienced.

(An interruption: The men maintain a lively interest in me; in return, they insist on being heard, reminding me that listening is usually more important than talking. Reminding me, too, that I'm a priest.) But freedom depends, it seems to me, on the degree that one is possessed by the truth. Confronting truth is the state of being under siege and submitting to conquest as gracefully as possible. Such is the price of freedom—"the truth will set you free." Christ clarified and expanded this point in the hushed atmosphere of the Last Supper—the disciples would receive truth in accepting him, not only the Father's image, but the real image of man. When one accepts Christ humbly and without qualifications, one stands against the personal and social lie—the "world's truth"—both in oneself and in society.

Martin Buber, in a commentary on Psalm 12, writes of what he calls the "generation of the lie." The lie in this generation has reached the highest level of perfection as an ingeniously controlled means of supremacy. "This generation" is every generation, which can be counted on to perfect the lie insofar as the lie is needed to establish worldly power and maintain it securely.

Our country appears to need the lie now more desperately than in the past, simply because the power that unites our history is today more threatened by truth. Despite this conflict, it is now the ambition of power to create a new hierarchy of supremacy, a new mode of exploitation. The West—and specifically the United States—is an innovator in this coldly gruesome task. Not by conspiracy, but by an inherent logic of survival. Wealth and privilege, almost synonymous for the West, had a need not only to expand themselves but also to protect their expansion against an increasingly resentful world. To this purpose, a new vocabulary has evolved. The illusions and distortions offered the American consumer have their counterpart in the propaganda offered the world. Both possess the same aim—

economic domination, which means, essentially, political and cultural domination as well.

It seems to me that the socialized lie—a war economy, imperialist ambition, institutionalized racism—can be confronted only by someone who has internalized truth and freedom. I have known many truthful men, but truth does not yet demand a severe social price in our society. Few of these truthful men could also be considered free; this is because they had not faced the public consequences of belief. This is a commentary on the subtle ability of technological man to divorce belief from life. Otherwise, I am convinced that "truthful" men would either be in jail or preparing to go to jail.

In his essay "On the Duty of Civil Disobedience" Thoreau comments on the scarcity of honest men. Interestingly, he does not restrict "duty" to ordinary citizens, nor does he imply that democracy is possible without citizens devoted to their duty of rebellion against unjust government. Of course, such a duty is almost never acknowledged by leaders of business, the church, the government, or—despite the Nuremberg trials—the Army. The best of them, in face of the most shocking and continual injustice by their government, will place their trust in reform, convinced that the dangers of change are far greater than the dangers of continuing present policy. But is not this another way of saying that personal benefit has become their overriding concern?

July 27

A priest writes, admonishing me to reject any bitterness at the treatment given me by my society, the Josephites, and by my bishop, Cardinal Sheehan of Baltimore. But I would be guilty of gross incompetence if I had acted without being thoroughly familiar with their scale of values and being able to predict their reactions. My correspondent, who is a theologian and professor, concludes his note with a reference to himself: "I'm raising hell with the Church in my own way." His whole assumption is that his ministry is to the Church. A good and earnest man, and not lacking in courage, he has dedicated himself to Church reform rather than to the service of man, his premise being that a liberalizing of dogma and discipline will turn the Church toward the world. Let us build true Christian community, he appears to say, and then we can build the body of man into Christ's Kingdom.

The Church, however, is not a community. It is a movement charged with preaching the Gospel, with announcing the Father's salvation through Jesus Christ. It becomes community not *a priori*, but only insofar as it repeats the saving act of Christ, a calling to truth, justice, and freedom—a calling to love. And it is a calling to martydom no less today than it was two thousand years ago; men will still murder Christians rather than endure true love from them. The crucifixion thus repeats itself.

My priest-friend respects my conscience, respects my opposition to warmaking and war, respects my presence in jail. And asks that I respect him and what he has done with his life. This I do, without agreeing with his conscience or where it has led him. In other words, I do not find his conscience particularly enlightened or his freedom particularly profound. He, and others like him, are interested only in an updated liturgy, clerical freedom to marry, and official approval for birth control. While the ship goes down.

July 28

My first visitors—members of my family—arrived for three hours this afternoon. Seeing them had special significance, because even some close friends have repeatedly been turned away. In any event, their visit communicates to me a blessing of freedom from my family, and a reminder of how ties of respect and love have deepened from that freedom. Given the need, I suppose that we would die for one another. But more importantly, we would die first for others who need us more. Given the need.

I have made my family suffer—not once or twice, but repeatedly. And in doing so, I have taken repeated cues from my brother, also a priest, and without reserve the greatest man I know. My parents, my brothers, and their families have by American standards a powerful right to something better. My family has made generous, if not extraordinary, concessions to the mystical union of God and country. Four sons went to war during the second world conflict—three of us served abroad in the Mediterranean and European theaters. Two sons are priests, another an outstanding educator and family man, two others the heads of superb families. And now this—one priest in jail and the other on his way. A paradoxical justice for my parents and the others.

Yet whatever one sacrifices conscientiously to justice is restored and renewed. So it has been with my family. There has never been a hint of reproof, much less of rejection. Only a strenuously loving effort to understand. And the result of this effort has often been to lead *me* toward deeper awareness of my special responsibilities.

That is why I say that our love for one another grows in intensity even as it grows in freedom. As we said our goodbyes, disconsolate parents and relatives were parting from their young men—criminals and inmates, as classified by the federal system. It was a moment sobered by the unmentioned possibility that I would never see my aged and feeble parents again. But we managed to preserve the essence of parting—refreshed by the strength we lent one another, and gladdened at the thought of the work yet to be done. Sadness and a sense of loss were clearly out of place. We left one another grateful for the mercy given us.

I am neither a sensitive nor a sentimental man. My background, experience, and discipline, the service that must be always available for others, have forced me to keep a tight rein on sentiment, to learn to master fear, and to adopt an attitude toward life which many would even consider reckless. A compromise with truth fills me with loathing, and an inability to conceal my position has sometimes made *my reality* painful to those I most love. But my family has smoothed the rough edges of arrogance, and their love leaves me a failure in love, and a debtor to it. Slowly, I am learning, and will continue to learn, that without love a passion for justice can fashion a demagogue and a brute. "Love takes no pleasure in other's sins, but delights in the truth; it is always ready to excuse, to trust, to hope, and to endure whatever comes." I Corinthians 13:6.

July 30

Slowly and tediously I have rewritten these notes. Eventually, some unfortunate friend will have to edit out their more boring and polemical elements.

I have never written well or easily—I have merely had aspirations to do so. To me there is nothing more exacting or laborious than writing. To compound such personal difficulties, there are the physical subterfuges that one must employ while writing in prison. Plus the lack of a typewriter.

I have heard writers say that longhand copy tends to involve them too deeply with their ideas, the product being overly personal and insufficiently objective. Without question, one's handwriting becomes a preoccupation and distraction, however slight; one cannot put it down and weigh it like a page that has been typed. However, I feel confident that jail experience will compensate for such defects, giving to content what might otherwise be lacking.

August 6

Today's feast is the Transfiguration of Christ; also, the twenty-third anniversary of the atomic attack on Hiroshima by our country. The two events, separated by over nineteen hundred years, have a terrible significance for each other.

In the presence of Peter, James, and John, the Father asserted that Christ was his beloved Son and commanded that we listen to Him. Hiroshima, in turn, asserted how much we had neglected—or refused—to listen. If anything can describe the nation's reaction to Hiroshima and the blast at Nagasaki three days later, it would be a massive sigh of relief based on a massive assumption: Some American lives and blood had been spared.

Such a feeling of relief was premature and illusory. No such security would ever again be experienced by our country or our world. As it happened, Hiroshima was the first military and diplomatic act of the cold war. The unspeakable violence with which it closed one world conflict immediately ushered in another. From that point on, the Russians had few reasons to trust us and many reasons to distrust us; while we distrusted them for reasons of both economic and ideological policy. The cold war began and has continued to grow—until one begins to feel oneself a witness to those "shortened days" of which we are warned in Scripture.

On August 6, 1945, I was safe in America, having recently returned from the war in Europe. My division had received orders to retrain for the invasion of Japan. The atomic blasts found me neither disturbed nor horrified, only vaguely disappointed that the armistice followed them a few days later. Like my countrymen, I was convinced of America's righteousness, just as I was convinced of my own righteousness in joining the fight. In other words, my criminal adolescence coincided neatly with that of my country.

Untried for war crimes like Hiroshima, we Americans felt guiltless. There was, in fact, no country, nation, or alliance of nations with the power to try us and to find us guilty. Only the dead and survivors remained in judgment. Now I have matured somewhat—with no credit to myself and with full credit to better people—matured to the point where I can say "No!" to Hiroshima and to many of America's policies, domestic and foreign, and live with my refusal, in jail or out. I have not lost confidence in my country; I have merely learned about it—this magnificent, frantic, insane nation-empire to which God has hinged so much of the future of mankind. Someone has said that if we knew the depth of our national corruption, we would in despair kill ourselves or flee abroad. But there are better responses to make, and Americans are making them. After all, there is no reason why a man should recoil more from his nation's sins than from his own; nor should it be impossible to understand how personal crimes can add up to—or cause—a CIA or a Viet Nam.

The elusive realities of such speculation, however, do not discharge us of responsibility for knowing things more concrete—that the United States, for example, has a quality of nationhood possible only because of our imperial successes. And our imperialist successes became possible because of our determinist attachment to laissez-faire capitalism. Any analysis of our excesses, whether of racism, the Robber Baron era, military interventions, or Open Door Policy, must come to grips with an expansionist economy— the soil from which most of our deadliest weeds have sprung. This helps us to understand how we could bomb a prostrate Japan to threaten Russia, our only serious rival in the post-war world. In this framework, too, we could maintain military missions in nearly a score of Latin-American "republics"; intervene in Santo Domingo and Viet Nam; conspire to overthrow progressive governments in Guatemala, Brazil, and Indonesia: and come to a nuclear face-off with Russia at Berlin, Suez, and Cuba. Indeed, our economic system, more than any single factor, has made Russia a minor-league facsimile of ourselves, with the same brand of raw ambition, ideological fixations, and saber rattling.

(Some have overly psychologized our tragic rivalry with Russia and decided that, needing a rival, we consciously created one: Since our aggressiveness overseas had to be made credible, a Russian threat neatly filled that role. The real processes at work, however, were hardly so conspiratorial. It is perhaps closer to the truth to maintain that our economy needed new outlets—into Eastern Europe, into Russia itself if we could get them. The effort produced a rival, but we intended nothing more than expansion. Most certainly we would have preferred not to have rivalry, preferring rather to have the whole world as open to penetration as was our West following the Civil War.)

A sober student will find it hard to avoid the conclusion that Americans have institutionalized war to maintain capitalist prosperity, and that institutionalized warmaking may now have a life of its own. A recent book forecasting future weaponry, *Unless Peace Comes*, edited by Nigel Calder (Viking, New York, 1968), predicts that, because of their wealth, the deep seas will become areas of international conflict. Gordon J. F. McDonald, a young American geophysicist, writes of a mass-produced manipulation of the environment, to cause catastrophe on command—violent windstorms, drought, frost, tidal waves—all as resources of the military arsenal. He also refers to the effect that weak oscillating fields can have on human behavior, observing that artificially induced lightning strokes can produce high power concentrations over certain regions. Thus a system can be created that would seriously affect brain performance; and for military purposes, such a system would preferably be employed in highly concentrated urban areas.

This inventory of civilized research does not stop there, nor can we suppose that its ghastly survey will serve as an adequate warning. A Nobel laureate physicist has reminded us that stopping weapons research is like stopping a war— it's easier to begin. "It's amazing how easy it is to find new and efficient ways to kill people if you put good minds to work on the problem."

Present bacteriological and chemical weapons are crude and wasteful compared with future counterparts; battlefield robots of ponderous power and indestructibility are being developed; military decision-making is coming to rely more and more on computerization. We can now look forward to the consequences of a computerized response to a computerized forecast of imminent enemy attack.

The weapons experts are specialists in a society dominated more and more by men like them, and less and less by humanists. How can they remain silent about those forces even now working toward the imminent employment of their deadly research? How can they remain so blind to the recurring pattern of imperial design, of wealth and power in the hands of fewer and fewer men, of warmaking as a process implicit in capitalist imperialism?

People must be helped to see that the elimination of institutionalized racism in the United States—that is, at a rate designed to forestall racial war and urban destruction— would upset the "balance of power" (a diplomatic term, by the way, newly applicable to domestic realities). By the same token, leadership in a bilateral shutdown of the arms race, in order to convert to the pressing demands of peacemaking, would "unbalance power" in favor of those not presently possessing it. Since power is not relinquished so reasonably or generously, since the capitalist nation of "self-interest" would thereby be jeopardized, power will probably grow in concentration, abuse, and threat. To the point of no return.

A study in contrast—the transfiguration of divine mercy on the Mount, and the transfiguration of human arrogance and pitilessness at Hiroshima. God struck his tent in Christ's human flesh, Whose shining face spoke—as long as it could endure—of divine power and compassion. While the fireball at Hiroshima consumed everyone it could reach, and blinded onlookers many miles away. It came, carefully stamped, "Made in U.S.A," a curious response by allegedly Christian people to the Father's imperative, "Listen to him!"

Can a nation recover from a mental lapse like Hiroshima, or more fundamentally, from a disintegration of humanity that made Hiroshima a fateful climax of moral bankruptcy? One can only hope that it can, while remaining aware that our indemnities to Japan have included making her the West Germany of the Pacific—a base from which to exploit the economies of the Far East. Meanwhile, our restitution to humanity for that unprecedented offense was an example of combined hypocrisy and threat, of freedom and over-whelming military power. Which is to say that our choice of transfigurations has not changed, almost as if what we are really at war with is the divine mercy itself.

August 9

I have been reading a series of essays on Latin America in *America* magazine (5/18/68). They focus on Pope Paul's encyclical "Populorum Progresso" and understandably have much to say about violence and revolution in reaching the goals of the Pope's message.

One article deserving special comment is by Bishop Marcos McGrath. On the one hand, he admits that human misery has approached a critical point in Latin America, but on the other hand he insists that a solution of violent revolution is morally reprehensible and politically self-defeating.

Few Latin Americans will oppose his first point, but many, including some of his episcopal colleagues, will take energetic exception to his second. One cannot so easily reject violent revolution as a means of redress while clinging to the adage "development is peace." How can development take place without self-determination, and how is self-determination possible under governments with military overtones dominated by foreign interests, mostly American? In a word, how is peace possible when justice, the instrument of peace, is denied?

"Revolution" is today the most feared, and consequently the least understood, word in our vocabulary—for most of us, apparently, it connotes all kinds of dark and devious assaults on privilege and power. Even Christians add their own anxieties and confusions to a concept which should give insight to their understanding of and dedication to the Gospel. In fact, "revolution" is an eminently Christian word which should guide all Christian response to human process. Revolution may be unchristian in certain instances, but a man cannot be a Christian without being a revolutionary.

Christian revolution means conversion to a crucified and risen Lord—and witness to this conversion. The Christian in the world faces in himself and around him the identical forces that make most institutional power a friend of few and the enemy of most. The "world," as the Gospel sees it, is a malicious force, both personal and social, an individual and collective psychosis that alienates the self and exploits the brother. In this view, war, racism, and poverty can be traced to our desire to avoid the cross that is part of life, thereby "preserving one's soul by losing it."

The "new man," who emerges slowly through conversion to the Christ of Calvary, rejects his own alienation by confronting the injustices of organized alienation, the institutions of power. For his efforts, he is duly "hated": "The world will hate you, because it knows neither the Father nor me"—and his lot becomes as bad as or worse than that of the victims he defends.

It is at this critical point, when a man experiences his Calvary in the form of ostracism, betrayal, jail, or a bullet, that he gives up his soul, to have it restored to him reborn. At this point the death and resurrection of Christ become a living experience. In the process, although without knowing it, society gains a reprieve of punishment and a new opportunity for a life that is human.

Rebirth, however, owes itself to a conflict of powers, one moral, the other exploitative. One faces this conflict expecting to be a different kind of victor by being a different kind of victim. Thoreau, I think, caught a glimmering of this. In his contest with the state over slavery and the Mexican war, he wrote confidently, "Let us see who is the strongest." He undoubtedly believed that being right (just) carried with it an ultimate strength which a formidable state could neither intimidate nor defeat. Although the state could convict, sentence, imprison, and kill a just man, it could not defeat him. He also believed that the more a state manipulates its courts, fills jails with its best people, neglects its great men or conspires to murder them, the more it loses its legitimacy, its mandate from the people, its very hope for the future. Only the profound myopia caused by its injustice prevents the state from seeing this.

Nothing is more needed today than revolutionaries who begin by serving the people with dedication and fidelity, but gradually train themselves for whatever risks must be accepted on behalf of justice. Humanity may proceed at phenomenal rates, technologically, but it owes its most genuine progress to those who look beyond gains in productivity and industrial development.

In the deepest sense, the Christian is neither for nor against violent revolution; he transcends such a choice by his dedication to a more basic change, the spiritual revolution commanded by Christ. On a given occasion, he may tolerate and approve—but not actively join—a violent revolution, having judged that political and social injustice had reached insufferable limits, without reasonable hope of redress. Also, he may oppose revolution for moral and political reasons, weighing the dangers of moral irresponsibility, political demagoguery, or military terrorism in the process, or judging that the movement lacks strong popular support.

In any case, his Christian sympathies lead him to identify with those afflicted enough and desperate enough to rebel. Both intelligence and compassion tell him that people do not rebel when they already have what their neighbors justly supply. Nor do people rebel for trivial or imagined reasons—not when the cost of failure is death. But they *do* rebel for reasons entirely different from those for which they are opposed.

Moreover, historical sense tells the Christian that violent revolutions backed by popular support have often produced human progress, that the violence during and after them has rarely matched the violence preceding and causing them, and that the respect accorded life by revolutionaries is vastly superior to the contempt given it by tyrants.

In fact, the Christian has reason to suspect that mankind is not yet capable of a better solution to the problem of entrenched, oppressive power than violent revolution, and that without it technological democracy tends toward fascism. Indeed, only if the smaller nations appreciate their revolutionary rights, and energetically act upon them, challenging the world's domination by the superpowers, can mankind hope to avoid nuclear destruction.

In the last analysis, who can understand the fateful complexities of revolution, except the man who has submitted to it within himself? That is, one who has abandoned all claim to personal rights, while insisting upon them for others. No attitude is so instinctively resisted, but no attitude is so close to the human helplessness of Christ in his Passion. If attention is also called to one's own personal rights, it is to remind the oppressor of his responsibilities in justice. "If there is something wrong in what I said, point it out; but if there is no offense in it, why do you strike me?" (John 18:23) But if the Christian refuses to vindicate his human rights for personal benefit, it is because the Lord refused such ambiguous human protection, giving evidence that only truth and love do God's justice to all. They alone lay bare the depths of the problem, probing the very heart of the persecutor, giving it an opportunity of repentance, light, and growth. To possess enough faith to act in such a way is a singular and undeserved gift, which men less blessed can only partially comprehend. They need their rights, their freedom to express them, and a visible response of justice. But they also need men of faith to take up their cause in conscience, even at the cost of freedom and life.

One final point. Those Christians who fear violent revolution—the Pope included—but do not attack the atrocities of the rich or suffer with the poor, ought at least to have enough humility to remain silent. They have not earned the right to pontificate or condemn. Indeed, they should take care that their action is not that of some who are content to watch a friend submit to degradation or death, after warning him of the immorality of resistance. Such an attitude is tantamount to a death sentence, a judgment which they themselves would probably reject. If they believed sufficiently in the immorality of violent revolution, they would be the first to accept death in order to remove the conditions on which it breeds.

Let the twenty percent of those Americans who have incomes of less than three thousand dollars a year, and the eighty percent of those in the Third World who live on less than three hundred dollars a year, decide what revolution fits their needs. Let others remain silent, or if they pretend to the name of Christian, let them give their support to the decisions of the poor. In this way, perhaps, they may atone in part for their previous silence and cowardice.

August 14

Billie is what I would call a street savage, and what jail-house veterans would call a hustler. Out "on the street"— prison parlance for freedom—Billie is a small-time con man living by the craft and ethics of the small-time underworld. Jet black, with a head massive and handsome, features shifting graphically from suspicion to cunning, a body kept lean and muscular by hyperactivity, he lives here as he lives outside, a professional in deals and dupes. But Billie also is a parasite, created by black-white syndromes and by that species of larceny we call profit motivation; pressed, he will admit being a small-time thief—he wants a piece of the national action.

Close observation of Billie reveals that he lives perpetually close to instant rage. Although he is not a big man, the impression he conveys is that of a spring coiled for hap-hazard destruction. For Billie "makes it" by menace—menace called upon and communicated instantaneously by expression, word, or gesture, each quickly convincing and credible. His features work and his hands fly about expressively, even convulsively, while his voice pours out a stream of obscene, incoherent, and defiant words. I have seen new inmates sit around Billie by the hour, fascinated, while he alternately played crime lord or black revolutionary. Finally they would leave stunned—all of them impressed by his singularity, most of them convinced of his madness. Yet their attention would encourage Billie, and he would go happily off to play harder games with older inmates.

Billie is, I'm convinced, a casualty par excellence of our white supremacist, hedonist, and manifest-destiny Great Society. If he is redeemable (I'm sure he is), he may very well be irremediable. Illiterate, ignorant, yet profoundly sensitive, he knows little except the tools of his trade, and the survival they supposedly guarantee. On the street, he pimps for white or black "Dudes," pushes narcotics or numbers, plays assorted con games with unwary tourists, gambles with cards or bookmakers. He loves life outside as passionately as he hates it here, perfectly unconscious that his profit schemes are played by respectable fellow countrymen with far greater impunity and success.

My coming opened new doors for Billie's trade. He introduced himself by offering labored and absurd evidence of devout Catholicism. When this was solemnly accepted, he swept into fond reminiscences of the old home town, after which he generously offered himself as my prison patron and bodyguard. "Don't nobody mess with Pop," he would scream to anyone within earshot.

Such security, however, came with a price tag. Soon he was confiding his financial embarrassments—this one or that one at home failing him, or money forever on the way. I believed him—as far as it went, he spoke the truth. (And of course there are many men here with neither families nor friends. Some do hard and valuable work for the institution, with little or no recompense.)

Soon Billie began to ask for cigarettes—jailhouse currency —and I responded by buying him a carton every other week at the commissary. (No easy trick, with other men in need, and a twenty-dollar monthly limit.) The arrangement proceeded happily, with enrichment to our friendship. One morning, however, Billie came to me in a rage. Someone had stolen his cigarettes, and because he is a heavy smoker, the theft had left him in painful circumstances. He was a consummate actor, ranting with such conviction and energy that he convinced me thoroughly. It was easy for me to feel sympathy for him, because with men largely defenseless and commonly poor, stealing in jail is a particularly despicable crime. It is, in fact, the capital offense, taken more seriously by inmates than an unjust attack, or even knifeplay.

Billie vowed to kill the thief and announced at large the traps that he would set for him. This should have made me suspicious—he was obviously protesting too much. But to my relief, his fury subsided after a half-hour, and I proceeded to think no more of it.

Tranquillity was short-lived. Coming in from the farm that evening, I discovered that I had become Billie's partner in fate, two cartons of cigarettes having disappeared. (Prior to their loss, I remember feeling guilty about such wealth, but men had returned loans, leaving me the lot of the rich, and ripe to be plucked.)

Events took a more rapid pace. The loss was of no great importance to me. I reflected that a type of justice had been served, since I had more cigarettes than I could possibly use, while others around me had none. Yet I compounded previous mistakes by mentioning the theft to Billie, who publicized it with evangelical fervor, taking special pride in his being a fellow victim. In an hour's time the news had penetrated to all quarters—apparently even to the administration. People came by to express their shame and regret. A few offered cigarettes; others brought locks and advice to use them.

My embarrassment and feeling of inadequacy poorly prepared me for what followed. Jailhouse justice began to take over. A delegation approached me with the stolen cartons, and one member, a huge black, confessed that he had won them gambling with Billie, and that news of the theft confirmed his suspicions that my friend had stolen them. I insisted that he take them back, but he vehemently and somewhat ominously refused. My sense of foreboding suggested that the violence so senselessly begun might produce new victims.

My suspicions were not unfounded. When Billie returned from work in the kitchen, he faced a committee of justice that charged him with theft, sentenced him, and promptly executed sentence. Tender sensibilities like mine could only regard the proceedings with amazement and aversion. Nevertheless, although it was a kangaroo court enforcing vigilante law, in its own setting it was vested with a certain legitimacy and force. Billie was given a thorough beating, which was accompanied by fearful expressions of derision and contempt. The whole affair was over very suddenly, violently, and effectively—before I could even get on the scene. Perhaps it could be compared to the branding of Cain.

But Billie was resilient. He rushed over to see me, and it was clear that he blamed me more than his judges. He demanded to know who it was that had framed him. When I refused to tell him anything, he stormed away, still protesting his innocence. Since then, he has been more subdued and remote, having little to say to me. Or I to him.

A staunch believer in human rights and compensatory treatment for blacks, I had contributed to this affair, unfortunately, more presumption than wisdom. In my paternalism I had judged Billie by an updated version of the white man's burden: Since he was ignorant, brutal, and neurotic, I would help him by an overwillingness to condone his failures, and an overavailability to his needs. In all honesty this is simply going one notch better than sitting in a rectory parlor dispensing sympathy, advice, and alms to "deserving Negroes."

I had forgotten that prison provides a common denominator for us, that previous credentials evaporated before that fact, or faced reevaluation and acceptance. And because I had forgotten, for Billie I became nothing more than another white "dude" ready for fleecing. Accordingly, his appraisal of me had been immeasurably more accurate than mine of him. He had set me up with relish; his only mistake was to gamble with the loot too soon.

Nevertheless, Billie himself remained the main victim. By offering him an easy touch, and in the process a temptation his greed couldn't resist, I had set him up and become an accomplice in a situation he was powerless to control. So he gambled, lost, was caught, and beaten, while earning the reputation of prison thief—a considerable liability.

Old hands here tell me, "Make many acquaintances, but pick your friends." It is unsatisfactory advice, typical of the rationale of survival that dominates prison life. I must try to keep enough perspective to be grateful to Billie, who taught me effectively and well. I should also be grateful that my helplessness kept me out of the way long enough to permit others to act. They alone were responsible for the meager benefits that resulted—a somewhat restored climate of justice, and a lesson for Billie that could probably not have been gained by more humane means.

Against advice, I will try to make many friends, including a few to confide in. Let me learn to serve the true interests of people, while letting them help themselves.

August 18

A welcome and captivating interlude. A young Jehovah's Witness strolls outside the recreation hall where I write, unconsciously serenading the sunshine, a few amused prisoners—and me. He sings a ballad of Bob Dylan and strums a guitar. Thank God, who has blessed us with troubadours, and with music of prophecy, hope, and renewal.

I notice a marked tendency among people who write—both friends and strangers—to feel sorry for me because I'm in jail. They show this by well-meant but excessive praise, and by their fervent prayer that prison doesn't make a sour and defensive cynic of me.

I wonder at such concern, even while treasuring the love that prompts it. What pain and uncertainty I've caused them: The pity they feel is a way of taking stock of their lives. Indeed, their doubts about me are a way of expressing doubts about themselves.

What doubts? one might ask. The people who bother to write are invariably men and women with a keen sense of justice; for them the suspicion that I have done the appropriate and just thing raises serious problems. It seems to me that this nation could do nothing better to awaken its conscience than to fill its jails with just men; in our present order, prison should be accepted and welcomed instead of being feared and shunned.

For me it is a rule that a man ought to test his life against events. The United States faces today a crisis of staggering proportions; some call it the worst since the Civil War; others, the most severe in our history. Many sober observers are convinced that we have entered that period of decline reserved for empires that are falling apart.

No one argues about the seriousness of the crisis, but most will differ about its character; in any case, our traditional institutions seem impotent before it. Business, for example, rejects both an equitable tax load and a curb on excessive profits; the military not only practices imperial terrorism but also influences high-level decision-making in domestic and foreign policy; the church, too, is seized with an unholy rage for law and order, while government continues to represent power rather than people.

Under neocapitalism, technology has been distinctly anti-humanist, tending to make our institutions at once obsolete and unrepresentative. Burdened with the same kind of determinist and relativist philosophy as the economic and political sectors that control it, technology has thus far served as a tool of power, more to be feared than welcomed. Indeed, our mechanical inventiveness has received, assimilated, and heightened the amorality of the society that patronized it.

Such a perspective appears to shed some light on the crisis gripping our society. We see the entirely traditional resolve of vested power to keep its crown and scepter— despite the "nay-sayers," as President Johnson calls them. Or, to put it differently, our foreign involvements and domestic crises imply an attempt by concentrated power to maintain high levels of active and subtle violence while "pacifying" both ideological opponents and victims. And the only novel aspect of this phase of imperial decline is its apparent inevitability in a nation allegedly democratic and unsurpassingly affluent.

When in a democracy reform begins to seem utopian, when election promises are neither honored nor kept—indeed, when they are sometimes never made—revolution beckons. President Kennedy once said that those who oppose peaceful revolution provoke violent revolution. We might keep that in mind when we hear the next politician exploiting popular fears with a ringing endorsement of "law and order."

September 9

A few more impressions of the scene. Harold Buchman (Baltimore attorney for the Catonsville Nine) came in tonight, and hopefully we'll start back to Allenwood tomorrow. September 12—still here. Weisgal (chief attorney for the Nine) called and promised to move the D.A. if he could. We'll look to Friday.

I miss the space at Allenwood, especially the opportunity

in its broad acres to think and reflect. A thirty-by-fourteen-foot cell is a departure from this, and more of an inhibition than I can tell you. Constant TV is a powerful invasion of one's silence. But all the noise here, and the impossibility to escape from it, reminds me that distraction is a profit item for many Americans and a social adhesive. It is one of our more treasured freedoms.

More than any others I know, the nine people who burned draft files at Catonsville can claim to be right in what they did, and dare to publicize that rightness. Of course, many will find this smug and arrogant, but I am not saying it because they were with me or I with them. Their choice was as mysterious as their right to speak is certain; their claim is that of justice, because their vision dramatized the crisis of injustice besetting America.

They saw their country maintaining its colossal affluence at the expense of other men, leaving warmaking as its largest industry and racism as its chief social attitude. Propaganda had replaced truth, and Hiroshima and nuclear brinkmanship seemed to be its testament to mankind.

Recent events have verified a diagnosis of vast power run subtly amok, incapable of recognizing its own sickness—and, therefore, incapable of change. Miami, the Viet Nam–Czechoslovakia parallel, the Chicago convention, the futility of choice between Humphrey and Nixon, law and order as *the* campaign issue—all provided similar evidence of the nature of the crime. Meantime, the waste in Viet Nam escalated, completely unaffected by the burlesque of "peace negotiations" in Paris. Our country's violence has a determinist momentum that creates obstacles without and erosion within.

There is more to command these nine—their vision had consistency, suggesting a way of life uniting personal relations and public responsibility. I have every confidence that their witness will remain steadfast and their example will provide ennobling resources to others.

In contrast, I have seen antiwar people, even those of sufficient moral conviction to accept jail, whose vision weakened under the experience. Each case stands individually, and all of these men deserve public gratitude. Nevertheless, in one instance, conviction apparently was exhausted with refusal of military service; in another, it ebbed away in loneliness and bewilderment; in a third, it seemed unconnected to political content and effect. Draft resisters have been all too apt to retreat into themselves or form little insulated groups, blind and unresponsive to people around them. Many of them would mark calendars until their release, hoping to normalize their lives outside; some even came to prefer "parole" into the Army rather than jail, which began to seem only a waste of time and political folly. A few, however, saw resistance as an obscure yet giant step into life, one to be pondered and enlarged. "The sower went out to sow his seed . . . some fell upon good ground."

What tainted the vision of antiwar men sometimes to the point where they seemed to lose it quickly and completely? They were rare men, a tiny handful whose fragile opposition kept madness from becoming consensus. They had friends who fled to Canada, classmates who longed for suburbia, parents who disapproved anxiously, clergy who were opposed or suspicious—all vast burdens for young lives. Yet they stood fast, often alone, through trial and sentence— and were finally placed in jail. Having endured these trials, one would think that they could endure anything.

But this is a superficial view. Men tried by one fire do not necessarily withstand another. As lines hardened, America institutionalized its opposition to their dissent, regarding them at best as unpopular, at worst as traitors. The nation felt no guilt in rejecting them, and promptly tried to forget them.

All this, of course, underscores how Americans fail to control their lives—or their government. History reveals us as a greedy and belligerent people—a fact that a horrified minority of intellectuals and students is learning only today. But dissent from government encroachment or tyrannical policy has never been a primary national value. Prosperity, not justice, is considered the basic function of government. Americans want help from their government in the intoxicating pursuit of wealth; and to further this goal, they are often prepared to brutalize the poor and to plunge vigorously into an unnecessary and unjust war. Sometimes we suspect that our wealth necessitates both poverty and war, but it would be unhealthy to develop scruples. When technology is joined exclusively to commercialism and war, the tendency to indict the dissenters is heightened.

With a culture centered on property and owing its spirit to profit-seeking, Americans usually think rather hazily about man, rather than concretely about the quality of man's life. We easily fall into the familiar "inclusive-exclusive" "me-or-you" pattern of the nineteenth-century nation-state, which our leaders readily adapted to imperial realities.

Marx, Malthus, and Darwin remain of critical importance in this regard, since the national rationale of "existence is survival" is derived directly from their writings. Both within and beyond the nation-empire, noncivilization waits as problem or threat—in Harlem, Berkeley, Appalachia, Viet Nam, Guatemala, and Biafra. In effect, we become a garrison that responds to one or a belligerent that attends to the other.

Fear, hate, and bewilderment deepen in our midst, while, slowly and inexorably, polarities continue to widen. Governor Wallace becomes as understandable a phenomenon as Vice-President Humphrey or Mr. Nixon. All have their constituencies. Wallace stands for lower-class whites—for little men who want an end to the threat from blacks wanting more elbow room at the national trough. Humphrey and

Nixon represent the elite, and those of the middle classes who identify with them—the rulers, financiers, and technicians of a neocapitalist empire. Issues have been reduced for all candidates to "who shall rule" and "who shall share." The reality of Viet Nam has not been allowed to intrude into the campaign, nor has the cold war, imperialist economics, or racism.

On the outer reaches of the struggle stands the unrepresented—blacks, poor people, some students, some intellectuals, a few of the clergy. They complain of the absence of justice and insist that if it is not to be a sham, it must be for everyone. Their attacks on reaction will bring about no sudden overthrow of bourgeois power, but a sustained campaign of nay-saying and disruption may slowly hammer out the concepts and institutions of a more human order. Early signs point to a model idealized by Cuba or North Viet Nam, rather than Russia or China. Presupposing, of course, that mankind avoids World War III.

Men still need to learn that excessive wealth, racism, and war mean the impossibility of a human, indeed a viable, society. Peace will remain an illusion until the atrocities of war and exploitation are eliminated. But it is only realism to recognize that their elimination will cost a terrible price in dislocation and suffering. And it will be the weak and the visionary who will suffer the most. Perversely, men have always valued their poor—valued them enough to insure that they will be numerous. And men have always punished their prophets. This is because the poor and the prophet force others to look at themselves in different mirrors, the former showing men as they are, the latter as they can be. Since both reflections are painful, both are hated, along with those who show them. When men no longer use their poor to exalt their own egos, when they no longer destroy their prophets, then justice will have come to the poor, and prophecy will be as treasured as power is now. Having

banished the ancient call to strife and blood, man can begin
to compete in love and service. Then we will begin to live.

September 12

"APOLOGIA FOR CAT"

"Humanity is skin deep in most of these guys—you'd better
believe it!" The guard spoke with conviction, and—I must
admit—a certain authority. He had broken up deadly fights
and legislated petty quarrels, had witnessed the effect of
racism and anti-Semitism, and he had tried to deal with the
daily routine of theft and homosexuality. Having often seen
men at their worst, and seldom at their best, he believed
thoroughly that their failures in prison were extensions of
their failures in society.

There was something in his remark, however, that was
deeper than observation—resentment at the thankless,
sterile job of a policeman. (American GIs in Viet Nam have
essentially similar feelings about themselves.) Even if he
did not explain the interplay of forces, he sensed that police
are caught in a frightening no-man's-land between rulers
and ruled; exhorted and criticized by one side, they are
hated and resisted by the other; their defense of the rulers
is at the same time oppression of the ruled.

Moreover, the bulging population of federal jails might
suggest a much more serious development than do statistics
about mounting crime—the readiness of police to identify
with oppression, to use force more and more arbitrarily, and
to unite informally with vigilante elements of the right. Apparently the police suspect that leftists may be right in
arguing that power ultimately means control of the army,
that the police are an occupation army, and that, therefore,
they are the first line of defense—and first target.

One must, nevertheless, be fair to the guards here. They

are, for the most part, uncomplicated and solid men—several being ex-farmers who still work little plots of ground. It is a tribute both to them and to an unusually sensitive warden that they consistently practice understanding and service to the men. A few are superb amateur psychologists who will amaze one with their offhandedly accurate judgments on prison mores. Among them I have often found compassion and a practical balance between harshness and indulgence.

"Humanity is skin deep"—the remark was significant, and I could not forget it. Moreover, an experience with an inmate forced me to ponder it at length and to wonder if it did not deserve to be applied to men at large, and to me particularly.

Marshals had moved Tom Lewis and me from the federal penitentiary at Allenwood to Baltimore County jail in preparation for our complex though legally hopeless trial. Room had to be made for us; consequently, while one guard processed us, another removed an inmate from a neighboring cellblock. The object was, of course, to keep us together; but however beneficial that might be to us, it was burdensome to the man moved, who was uprooted and forced to acclimate to new people and conditions.

Our addition brought the block to capacity—an effect like that of stacking Harlem liberally with refugees. To varying degrees, the territorial imperative went to work; old acquaintances greeted us with restraint, but strangers expressed more hostility than welcome. The reason was simple: Our arrival meant less room and less freedom of movement, plus the likelihood of abrasiveness and hostility. As newcomers we were sure to add burdens to backs already bowed!

One man (we did not know him) was called "Cat" or "Cotton," from his loose-jointed way of ambling around, and his taffy-colored kinky hair. He was light enough and Negroid enough to be a rare hybrid. (I thought upon seeing him that he could never "pass" and would often be a curiosity to his own people.) During our first evening here, we saw little of Cat, but heard him talking animatedly with another black youngster at the end of the cellblock. I remember the suspicion that they were "up tight" with one another and that the old racist themes were openly at work.

After lights out, however, our real initiation to Cat began. For something close to an hour he tormented us with a series of weird and prolonged cries, which our astounded and unaccustomed ears could not distinguish as laughter or crying. I lay in the bunk above him desperately trying to fathom this new phenomenon—had Tom or I provoked him in some way? Was this a new kind of emotional safety valve? Were these cries born of despair? Was he simply mad? Whatever the case, he finally grew weary and fell asleep, leaving me to an uneasy doze and more questions than answers.

Next morning I asked one of the whites what "gave" with Cat. His answer was contemptuous and abrupt: "Hell, he's on his way to Pawtuxet!" (A state mental institution.) The manner of delivery indicated that the sooner Cat left, the better the speaker would like it.

That evening, verifying my worst fears, a similar performance began. Nerves were taut by now—I had noticed during the day how preoccupied and touchy the men had become, and helplessness had exaggerated my own irritation. Consequently, after another period of this unearthly howling, my patience evaporated and with scarcely controlled anger I ordered Cat to stop his mad noise and to allow others to sleep.

Now, we had with us in jail a cab driver—let's call him Jensen—jailed on the fantastic charge of raping his common-law wife. No one could have been less equipped for jail—he had a bad ulcer and enough hypertension to keep it bad; he could neither sleep at night nor stomach the coarse, starchy food. He was hardly an attractive figure, constantly repeating his story, whining and complaining as if the only problem in the world was his. But when his hands trembled more day by day, and he confided to me over and over that if he were not released on bail he would crack up, several of us asked the guards to get him to the hospital. They, however, apparently thought that he would adapt; as one said to me, "People in here gotta adapt. Jensen'll make it!"

Jensen didn't make it. The night in question, when I told Cat to shut his mouth, he was pacing our tiny cell, chain-smoking begged cigarettes. (There is something eerie about a man pacing in an eight-by-eight-foot cell while three others attempt to sleep. On two earlier occasions I had been shut in with men on cold turkey, a witness to their terrible nausea, muscular constrictions, and insomnia. They would pace up and down, do deep knee bends, retch, and try to sleep; finding this futile they would get up and repeat the performance.)

Despite Jensen's pacing and mumbling, I fell asleep, where-upon Cat, doubtless furious because of my rebuke, turned upon Jensen, reviling his ancestry, morality, and his whole life, while repeatedly threatening to beat him. When I awoke for breakfast, Jensen was cowering at the end of an upper bunk, a big, frightened rabbit. Later he told me of the night's terror, and sobbed at the memory of it. Suddenly, the last remnants of control vanished; trying to restrain him was like trying to hold a pet bear when it first smells the forest. Then the guards came, he quieted down, and they led Jensen away. It was the last we saw of him.

Since Jensen was both helpless and harmless, Cat's per-secution of him seemed the worst depravity. My resentment was encouraged by the continuing campaign against me. He slept most of the day and was awake most of the night, when, between spasms of mad laughter, he would whisper stealth-ily from the lower bunk, "Devil, devil, devil, devil!" and,

"Go, go, go!" At those odd moments when he was awake during the day, he would steal a glance at me, look quickly away, and explode into wild sobs. He would take my slightest word or gesture, and mimic it for the general enjoyment. There was a request to have him moved, but the guards refused, suspecting that Cat wanted to avoid charges by pretending derangement. We had told them nothing of Jensen's persecution, and they apparently wanted us to handle Cat. "He's your problem," they said.

He was, indeed. What frightened me most was the fact that I was beginning to share his violence. He was no physical match for me, and if it ever came to a fight, I was sure I could hurt him badly. Therefore, I waited for a chance to challenge him and to bring affairs to a climax. A brief struggle, I surmised, and it would be over; he would be educated and I would be relieved. Anything seemed better than what was happening. On three occasions it nearly came to such an end, despite the fact that I was aware of the consequences —denial of the Gospel and nonviolence, exacerbation of black-white relations in jail, scandalous conduct for a priest, possible serious physical harm to another man.

I was nearly helpless before my anger—all the discipline of the years, all the fine, sensitive convictions I had learned from books and friends, were forgotten. Trapped by a giant primitivism that I could neither understand nor cope with, I was simply helpless to pursue alternatives that would break the vicious stalemate between us. I could not bear to speak to him, to take him casually or jokingly, to have the slightest normal thing to do with him. The only communication between us was his readiness to harass me, and mine to break him if the occasion offered. It was a murderous impasse, making a mockery of my thirteen years of work with black people.

The danger is over now. It probably wore itself out from its own inner fury. I deserve no credit for the change, except that somehow I found the strength to control myself. It is now possible to see more clearly what Cat is about, and what I am about. The former gives me hope, while the latter appalls me—which may be a healthier state of affairs than before.

Regarding what Cat is about. He is obviously two things —young and black. This society has turned off his youngness and his blackness—perhaps irrevocably. He lived in a slum created by whites, he faces charges for white man's work (armed robbery); he stagnates in a white man's jail. While here he must submit to white control, eat vapid white food, and watch the idiocy of white commercialism and violence on TV. He had little choice about such realities—Cleaver would call him a field nigger and field niggers have no choices. All the same, he is a bright and sensitive young man, with considerable Muslim influence in his background. (Hence, the "devil, devil" bit.)

Nevertheless, is he a madman, or simply an antisocial force as this society defines one? (Yesterday he smashed a young white into our cell bars, opening a head wound requiring seven stitches. This morning, with no apparent provocation, he jumped another youngster, and I had to haul him off. Not surprisingly, the guards found these assaults sufficiently dangerous to move him to another cell.) Gandhi maintained that it is better to resist injustice by violent means than not to resist at all. What alternatives were possible? To require nonviolent resistance from him was absurd in light of the passive violence forced upon him, and how could he listen to those who were accomplices in his treatment? Consequently, he replied to the abuse received in the same coin in which it was offered. And though the current objects of his violent resistance (us) might be clumsily and indiscriminately chosen, what others were available? The fact that he lashed out blindly is no argument for his submission.

Rather, it seemed to me that he was obedient to a deeper rationality than the one society would have him learn. Life "in the street" could have forced him to far deeper madness if he had submitted to it without active question, to be ruined by it and flung aside like a filthy rag—as many of his people had been ruined and flung aside, their misery serving only to increase the arrogance and affluence of their masters. I suspect that Cat sensed something of the ruthlessness with which this nation intends to remain white supremacist, oligarchical, and exploitative, and decided he should stand firm in his resistance, by whatever means.

Hence the separatism he practiced in jail was not purely a racist reaction. It was more a quarrel with a society that he believed to be mad, and whose madness he had to resist. And if he met people here who shared his resistance but not his means, how was he to understand?

As for what I am about, this is a far more subtle question, largely excluding the assumptions and conjectures one employs with others. But I did learn something about myself. The cold impersonality of the system could jail me for crimes against it (translate "crimes" as moral acts against its law), and I felt little resentment or bitterness. But let another person trample on me, and I am neither ready to offer the other cheek nor to walk the other mile. Rather, I am ready for violence. And this seems to be not only because the psychology of power is easier to understand than the psychology of a person, or because institutional violence is easier to understand than interpersonal violence, but because dealing with the former demands far less discipline and creativity. The exercise of power is simplified in its institutional form by the unfreedom of its supporters; on the interpersonal level every human person is a universe.

Because our understanding of others is so profoundly inadequate, we have only proportionate ability to absorb the others' violence. I recall an incident when a black man

bitterly cursed me out on a Baltimore street because I had
cut him off in traffic. I got out of the car, shamefacedly took
his tongue-lashing, and apologized. I was wrong, I had done
him an injustice—this was something I could *understand*.
But what of an occasion when one is right and another is
wrong; when another does in fact persist in the role of the
enemy? In a sense, one's territory has been occupied and, if
we can believe what Lorenz says about human aggression,
there are no inhibitions (as in the animal world) keeping
us from retaliation—even to the point of slaughter.

Every man is a missing link between lower forms and
higher life; between the primordial swamps and the heights
of selflessness. And though at present we seem intent upon
organizing the ordnance of mass murder, the fullness of
time has been established by the fullness of man in God's
own Son. If man is in the process of growing up in Christ,
must not his moral law be growing up as well? This is not
to question the law of love as God's covenant with man, but
an attempt to give reasons why we must live by that covenant and to regret our failure to do so. But hope endures.

September 19

People tend to think, almost automatically, that when a
lawyer takes a case it is because his client has a problem.
It is assumed that people in legal difficulties are in the same
relation to their lawyers as patients to doctors, penitents to
confessors, and drivers to mechanics. The common view
holds that a person approaches such professionals because
they can mediate for him in terms of need—pain, authority,
malfunction, and so on.

We have experienced something different, however, perhaps to the point of paradox. Furthermore, attempts at
explaining the paradox tend to remain superficial and stereotyped—reflecting both semantic and cultural problems. This

is partly because when a man goes to jail on behalf of people
(including himself), personal burdens have lost significance,
while universal burdens have increased in importance. Or
because the "I" has grown to mean less, and the "we" more.
Or because one has sensed "the inner order" of things, crav-
ing further familiarity with it. But this is an order which
legality and lawyers can seldom understand and almost
never defend. As the district attorney remarked in an un-
guarded moment during the Customs House trial, "The law
is completely unequipped to judge morality, or moral men!"
This leads to a claim to be made humbly yet persistently:
We serve our lawyers much more than they serve us. Indeed,
the witness we have so hesitantly accepted would be profoundly contradicted if it were otherwise. Lawyers offer us
their services spontaneously and generously. And we accept
in the same spirit because we know that we stand for them,
as well as for others; we have in effect taken their place.
They suspect this now, and in their candid moments they
might admit it, as others have. Several people wrote us after
both the blood-pouring and napalming incidents, "Thank
you for acting for us!"

A subsequent experience might make this clearer. Following our sentencing in May, 1968, for the blood pouring, a
variety of visitors—friends, curiosity seekers, and a few disturbed people—descended upon the county jail seeking Tom
Lewis and me. Facilities for visiting have been improved
since, but they were atrocious then—a tiny slot of a room
fitted with low benches, ugly waist-high grilles the size of a
cigar box, surmounted by a plate-glass window. "A visit,"
as the inmates called it, meant shouting into the grille and
fighting to hear your visitor's shout—all in angry competi-
tion with the unhappy people flanking both sides of the glass.

Two hours of this three times a week was hot and frus-
trating work, particularly in the face of lack of comprehen-
sion, misplaced pity, and the sheer labor of communicating.

Because I am a priest, people looked on me with a mixture of adulation and incredulity, as though I were a kind of political Padre Pio. Because we were Catholics, people wanted opinions on anything from birth control to Archbishop Cooke to symbolic civil disobedience. One saucer-eyed little college girl inquired despairingly, "What I can't understand is: Why napalm?" After one particularly numbing session, Tom Lewis remarked cryptically to me, "They think they're doing the works of mercy, but we end up serving them."

So it is with our lawyers. Their moral convictions assume that defending us is their share of justice. But they will probably discover that such a supposition is far wide of the mark.

Many may recoil from a bald assertion like that. I make it, however, not to label them cowardly and us courageous, but to illustrate the meaning of our resistance. We have withstood illegitimate power, attacking its militarism, racism, and false prosperity with noncooperation in word and deed. Moreover, we claim to have done this completely according to the letter and spirit of nonviolent civil disobedience.

It is critical to remember that power is less likely to become illegitimate if it is not bureaucratized. Moreover, once it becomes illegitimate, power can possess neither credibility nor sanction if law does not protect its bureaucratic operation. Thus, in both Viet Nam and Czechoslovakia, propaganda has attempted to promote a kind of situation-legality, as contrived as it is unreal. In matters crucial to its own survival, therefore—that is, matters affecting its wealth and popular support—illegitimate power will manipulate the law, make it (if need be), enforce it, and crush any threat to it.

In this sense, the law partakes of illegitimate power, for just as propaganda ensures its credibility, the function of legality is to gain public sanction for it. Consequently, this administration will make a great show of tolerating verbal dissent. At the point of pantomime, however, free speech ends. The administration will harass large protest assemblies with police power, while those who practice civil disobedience can be sure of a "fair" trial and a long jail sentence. In a word, government will use proportionate suppression against any threat. And with a swollen overconfidence, it fully expects to prosecute its wars, run its empire, and keep its home plantations quiet. So far it has done all three, a notable achievement.

When it comes to defending political dissenters like ourselves, lawyers become accomplices in the game against us —if, that is, they play its rules. They unite with the criminality of the bench in what is called a court of justice—a monstrous euphemism, indeed. Belief in the law is no adequate excuse for this. We, too, believe in the law, but we do not believe in those who manipulate it to favor warmaking, white skin, wealth, and privilege against the poor. (To us, such legal manipulators differ little from those illustrious founders of America's foremost families, with their robber baron giants of industry and finance: Gould, Vanderbilt, Morgan, Carnegie, and Hill.)

This is not to say that we expect lawyers to quit or to join us. But we do expect them to realize that, so long as it sacrifices justice, law will never be an instrument of order. We also expect them to realize that such a sacrifice of justice is precisely what makes power illegitimate.

We also expect them to abandon their naïve conviction that illegitimate power can reform itself through a combination of internal goodwill and legal dissent, whether domestic or foreign. To exemplify the first, I would mention a high Defense Department official's emotional remark to me, "The thing that most keeps me on this job is what some s.o.b. could do with it if I were out!" And the second, an opinion offered me by a congressman friend, "Unless the people give us some leverage, we're helpless to act!"

Both views are massive fallacies. Illegitimate power subtly or crudely corrupts the most honest of men, if for the simple reason that it doesn't allow public honesty. (Witness Stevenson, Goldberg, and now Ball at the UN. President Kennedy reportedly called the first "my official liar at the United Nations.") Illegitimate power simply grows defensively paranoid at legal dissent, as Chicago has most recently proved. What our lawyers, along with other American liberals, must learn is that illegitimate power can protract the Viet Nam war indefinitely, despite majority opposition, can escalate the cold war as it chooses, and can crush any ghetto uprising with impunity. To keep dissent within legal bounds is actually to join the insane rush of illegitimate power toward mass destruction.

These are harsh lessons for lawyers, but they are beginning to seep in. One man vacillates between a possible move to Israel—"the U.S. has too many insoluble problems!"—and the astonishing belief that he will win an appeal for us. As yet, apparently, he sees no contradiction between the two. Recently he asked me, "What would you think if we won our appeal?" I told him that if that happened I would try to discover what was wrong. Such men and institutions, so profoundly entrapped in corporate exploitation and horror, can, at best, master duplicity. I remember a great fear seizing me when Johnson announced that he would not run for the Presidency and that he would restrict the bombing of North Viet Nam. Something, I felt, was definitely wrong.

In our first trial, both judge and prosecutor—they operate as a unit against political defendants—charged us with arrogant contempt of the law. We felt, as they said, "above the law." Their language was the language of guilty and frightened men, but it was also the language of bureaucratic

sycophants who had digested thoroughly their lessons from the powers at the top. They knew its metabolism and loved its favors—so well, in fact, that they could treat its critics like personal enemies.

We are their enemies, but not in the sense that they imagine. In reality, we are their best friends—if they want to consider themselves guardians of the law, let them learn that the law responds to principle before power, to human need before vested interest, to morality before pragmatism. Let them understand that the law they represent has fallen into disrepute, not because people are especially irresponsible and lawless, but because the law has become a field manual for naked power and a club against the poor.

If they would be lawyers, we would also want them to be men. There is no good reason why lawyers cannot attempt in political cases what nonviolent revolutionaries are accomplishing in the streets—namely, the embarrassment and exposure of illegitimate power. There is no good reason why lawyers defending an antiwar case can't realize that a guilty verdict has been passed before the trial begins, and that they are morally obligated to dramatize such a colossal effrontery to justice. There is no good reason why there should not be as many lawyers in jail for contempt of court as there are young men imprisoned for draft resistance. The expression of such a conviction seems to me the only way to restore honor to a profession which today is nearly as dishonored as the priesthood.

If events are any index, wealth and power, as they are now conceived and administered, are obsolescent. So is the law. For me there is no serious alternative to confronting their injustice, inviting their repression, and accepting jail as the first of *their* major defeats. Spiritually, this means to dare human renewal; socially and politically, it means to feed a revolution. Like other Americans, our own lawyers

will receive invitations to the banquet. It will be to their credit to accept them, and to be the first of their profession to put on a wedding garment.

September 24

I've just read Eldridge Cleaver's *Soul on Ice*, which an unusually accurate dust-jacket blurb calls "one of the discoveries of the 1960's." Providentially, Cleaver's book reached me during a period of jailhouse doldrums, when existence passed for living, and living was about as appetizing as unseasoned oatmeal. Oddly enough, neither depression nor self-pity was the trouble. Rather, it was a kind of moral exhaustion, which reduced reality to an obscure and vapid common denominator. Somehow, neither the world, nor people, nor jail stimulated me, and I seemed powerless to turn them on. For a time, at least, dullness and lethargy had their day.

Yet Cleaver snapped me out of it with his lucidity and outrage—a rare combination, deplorably lacking in what masquerades as social criticism today. It was Simone Weil, I think, who observed that truth creates its own room, as though to take possession of a person. Cleaver provided such a service, dispelling the vacuum within me. As fundamentalist Christians would put it, "He performed a ministry for me."

Many things about this book moved me. In general, it is a raw and slashing attack upon American life, while preserving a delicate balance of humanity and humaneness. Cleaver never insists that whites become more than he has become or that humanity is less possible to a white racist than to a black man. No one can discount the obstacles he faced and overcame—poverty, blackness, and a brilliance whose misguidance in early life made him a racist and a brute. "If I had not been apprehended [for rape of whites]," he says, "I would have slit some white throats."

Once back in prison, he began to write, hoping to capture an identity that he had never really had. Writing forced him to read, and brought him to the conclusion that life meant more than what he knew of himself and of white America. From that turning point, he began to build an authentic humanity, as *Soul on Ice* testifies.

While not desiring to make this a book review, I can't resist the opinion that Cleaver's grasp of racist psychology is as incisive as Baldwin's but more comprehensive. He sees correctly that ghettos create both the black colonist and the black mercenary—abject caricatures forced upon black Americans at home and abroad. To Cleaver "separate but equal" for black in the United States equals "Open Door" foreign policy; he understands that the Great Society has only faintly and grudgingly upgraded "separate-but-equal" opportunities and facilities, and that, like foreign aid, these slogans represent a disarming attempt to disguise control of other human beings.

Fortunately, Cleaver's book, along with a few similar studies, is beginning to convince many people—particularly the young—that there is only one policy governing America's national and international life, a policy precisely tailored for expansionist capitalism. That is, it is tailored to enrich further a predatory wealthy elite and to solidify the position of a somnolent middle class, which serves in effect as a buffer to insulate the wealthy from change from "below."

Nevertheless, the impression that lingered after finishing *Soul on Ice* was simply the intense drama of a man liberated by the honesty of his suffering. Saint Paul has told us how Christ learned obedience through his suffering. Some might not think of applying this to Cleaver, but he strikes me as a man profoundly obedient to a truly human order—a man of acceptance as well as of determination. One does not develop such virtues except through suffering.

Malcolm influenced him tremendously; today's Black

Panthers are several logical steps beyond Malcolm's stillborn Organization of Afro-American Unity. When America grows up, it will treasure both men, who won their humanity in jail, and combined the roles of visionary and activist; one of them has been murdered, the other remains precariously alive, destined for leadership or a racist bullet.

But I need to explain about Cleaver's ministry to me. Despite freedom from many problems in jail, I am susceptible to one of the most common—tedium. Tedium feeds on drabness and routine; overcrowding, steel bars, and body counts; and isolation from community, issues, and struggle. In effect, tedium tempts one to quit; to submit gracelessly, and imperceptibly to "cop out"; to relish appearances rather than reality; to think less, feel less, and love less; to give up a living, growing Christianity for the duration.

Like most temptations that demean us, tedium fits in with what seems rather than what is. Applied to the jail situation, this means stressing confinement, bureaucratic rigidity, custodial impersonality, moral and political uselessness, the hang-ups of the inmates, the total climate of futility and waste. No wonder that prisoners "chalk off" that portion of their lives, as if it were empty of anything constructive. Extreme cases tend to despair: Since I've been there, one lad killed himself at Lewisburg—a long sentence and a burdensome confinement made him despondent—and powerless to cope with the news of a younger brother's death in Viet Nam.

Tedium is terrifying to me as a kind of deadly abrasive that works on a man's spirit like wind and water on loose soil. The erosion that results is very nearly inevitable. How depressing it is to see men of intelligence and accomplishment (who are not uncommon in federal prison), far more innocent of crime that many of our public pillars (not uncommon either), licking their wounds like punished children, feasting on distractions, and longing uncritically for a society which has misused them but which they intend neither to hold accountable nor to reform. I find myself trying to discover in them a spark of constructive anger, but all they seem to want after release is anonymity and normalcy.

Somebody has said that life consists of catching up with what one has done, or going beyond it. I feel that the first alternative applies to me, calling for a sustained pondering of what I have done, and a present consistent with it. Otherwise life might become a sterile compromise, setting at work a series of mysterious injuries among people depending on me. I have seen such compromises—and their effects— accepted by men who had acted courageously against injustice and never recovered from the consequences.

Life is more precious than liberty, and to offer up one's life is more difficult than to surrender one's property. But my conscience did not allow self-immolation, so I gave what was possible. Since resistance required trading liberty for imprisonment, imprisonment should be another way of extending resistance, and even of adding to it. Jail should provide the vantage point of being at the heart of moral conflict, yet physically detached from it; of being at grips with what Saint John calls "the world" (the institutions of domination), yet removed from public struggle with them.

To appraise my situation from a merely political view is to come close to destroying it. Friends commiserate with me and watch the political horizons anxiously, looking for a change of weather that would give strength to a legal appeal, or a better chance for executive clemency. They are sympathetic but not particularly perceptive. If I were the lowliest of draft resisters, buried anonymously in some federal prison, forgotten by everyone but parents and one or two friends, I would be contributing more to the building of peace than the most spectacular dove, who makes headlines and rallies supporters, and whose exhortations are heard with apprehension even in the halls of government. "Yet to shame the wise, God has chosen what the world counts folly, and to shame what is strong, God has chosen what the world counts weakness. He has chosen things low and contemptible, mere nothings, to overthrow the existing order. And so there is no place for human pride in the presence of God." I Cor. 1:27–29.

Yes, Cleaver has done me a service by giving me some of his strength. His fight for manhood gives energy to my own, since in every case that fight is an unfinished business. But one can face it better, knowing of another who had less to work with, and who became, in spite of that, a better man.

THE TRIAL

Nine people go to trial today—my brother Dan Berrigan, Tom Lewis, John Hogan, Mary Moylan, Tom and Marjorie Melville, George Mische, David Darst, and myself. All Catholics. We make the point of being Catholic because our Church has given us Christianity and because we hope to make it Christian. If that possibility lies within us.

This trial is another phase of resistance—as difficult in its own way as the napalming at Catonsville or prison itself. In court one puts values against legality according to legal rules and with slight chance of legal success. One does not look for justice; one hopes for a forum from which to communicate ideals, conviction, and anguish.

Our object is a short trial—intense, forthright, and dramatic. The government will prove what we already admit—destruction of draft files—while simultaneously excluding the "why" of burning them. It will charge that breaking the law is also a crime; we will maintain that breaking the law in the case at hand is no crime, but rather a moral and political duty. The government will assert that our motive

111

and our intent are one; we will reply that our motive was to destroy those files, and our intent was to illustrate the genocide in Viet Nam and the corruption of our country. It will make its laws an absolute; we will claim a higher law. (The government prosecutes us as they would, if logically consistent, prosecute a man for destruction of property because he broke down a door to save children in a burning building. We say that such a man deserves a medal.)

The prosecution hardly needs a strategy—it is that simple. It needs merely to establish beyond a reasonable doubt what we admit, and indeed, boast about. "People just can't take the law into their own hands!" The court is so blind as to exclude testimony about America's national and international illegalities—about ghetto despair, starving children, Viet Nam, Guatemala. Apparently, power can take the law into its own hands, a fact which the court refuses to admit. For if it did, what would happen to power stripped of the protection of law?

The determination of the prosecution, therefore, is to keep the law in the law's hands for the benefit of power, a determination that puts us under the law's power, and subject to its equivocal blessings.

Two huge American flags flank the judge's bench, their staffs adorned by brass eagles. Portraits of eminent jurists gaze down from the back wall with well-bred resolve, champions of the public interest. The wood paneling, lofty ceilings, and substantial furniture of the courtroom seem tasteless and affected, stamped with the pompous assumptions of an affluent society. Here privilege emphasizes its prerogatives and shields its interests. Noblesse oblige, I mutter cynically.

The long years of my devotion to the flag, to an unreflecting justification of law and order are before me, and I think back to the time when the exorcism of my soul began. When

I began to be less of a nationalist and more of a human being. It was like undergoing prolonged surgery, and just as painful.

Our lawyers sit a few feet in front—Bill Kunstler, famed for his defense of "controversial" figures like H. Rap Brown and the Black Panthers; Harrop Freeman from Cornell Law School; Harold Buchman, our local attorney; and Bill Cunningham, a Jesuit priest and law professor from Chicago. They are a brilliant and devoted group, capable of making us as secure as any lawyers can.

Harrop and Bill Cunningham have just arrived and must be sworn into the case. The court clerk charges them with conduct "consistent with truth and honor." Good enough—that shouldn't be difficult: they have come forward simply to defend men of truth and honor. Any attempt, however, to apply "truth and honor" more widely leads to semantic problems. What of the court's truth and honor, impossible to verify without impugning its own fidelity to unjust law, to the defense of its government and its government's wars? What of the future of this court because it chooses to make a farce of "truth and honor"? What adage best applies to it? "A house divided against itself will fall," or, "A house undivided by justice will fall."

The trial opens formally with "voir dire," or selection of jury. Which presents a very sensitive problem. How do we get twelve peers and hope for the infinitesimal chance of "hanging" them through one dissenter, in spite of the culling process that weeds out nonconformists and seats straight and sure people? Our peers include, as simple observation quickly confirms, no ghetto people, no students, no peaceniks or political radicals. They represent those on voting-registration rolls, with solid credit ratings, with Rotary Club, PTA, and Knights of Columbus membership. Would a real Christian have a chance of being selected?

In the Customs House trial, we gave in to legal naïveté

and endured three days of voir dire, involving 103 people. During this numbing process, we encountered one old man, disqualified by infirmity, who offered his opposition to the Viet Nam war in a quivering voice: "It should never have happened."

This time we assert our neutrality toward selection and force the government to select twelve men without challenge from us, thereby expressing our distrust of any jury named under the circumstances. Two hours later, a jury averaging fifty-five-years of age verifies our suspicions. They represent not the communities from which we come or which we serve, nor even a cross-section of the public, but simply the great spotless middle class, whose virtue lies in well-fed anonymity, daily deodorant, and Negro-Communist phobias. We look over at three men at the prosecutor's table, one of whom is an FBI agent who did the investigations of both the blood-pouring and napalming incidents. He will sit patiently through the whole trial, as though waiting for vindication of his skill, and the honor of the FBI. One of the other two men at the table, both assistant district attorneys, is a black named Murphy. We wonder if Murphy suspects that his blackness is a public-relations weapon in the government's hands to temper our human-rights convictions. Whatever the case, the district attorney appears confident enough to run the risk of using a second-string prosecution team.

Judge Thomsen presides—head magistrate of the Fourth Federal District Court. Typical of the WASPs who dominate the federal courts along the Mason-Dixon Line, he is a kindly, paternalistic figure, who on occasion will admit that he is out of his depth with us. His Honor will force from us a grudging respect by his quick realization that crisis has come before his bench, leaving him little time to understand it. Later, we will see him negotiate within the strict limits of his law, applying the spirit of American diplomacy:

Whom you can't control, negotiate. From strength, of course.

With two thousand demonstrators in the streets, and George Wallace coming to speak at the Baltimore Civic Center, the judge closes proceedings in midafternoon. His Honor has a full share of anxieties—a jury to get safely out to a hotel; order to be maintained in a courtroom packed with antiwar people; tremors from outside to be received, analyzed, and accommodated. All under the vigilant eye of thirty to forty press people.

Tuesday, October 8

With preliminary skirmishes over, Mr. Murphy outlines the prosecution case by telling the court what issues are not relevant. Conscience is not an issue; neither is morality or sincerity. Law and justice are not issues, the Viet Nam war is not an issue; neither is ghetto poverty, nor United States intervention around the world. The issue is simply whether we destroyed government property, whether we destroyed Selective Service files and hindered Selective Service operation. He brings forth a chart of the draft room at Catonsville and briefly points out what happened there. "The defendants pretend nonviolence," he says, "but they used force and violence here." He asks the jury to imagine what "effect this action would have on the operations of Local Board 33."

Bill Kunstler's opening statement exhorts the jury to decide not on facts, but on principle and intent. He reminds them that our prosecution is not as simple as the government pretends and that there are two paramount issues—what we admit doing, and why we admit doing it. We notice at this point that Kunstler is risking a contempt charge—the great fear of lawyers—since in a political case judges claim the power to exclude conscience as an influence upon intent. Judge Thomsen promptly intervenes by giving one of many preliminary instructions to the jury, whom he admonishes to make their decision on the evidence and what he says the evidence means. In a word, the jury must render a verdict purely from the law as against the events of May 17.

I sit there and think, "Here is the time machine cranking up again." Back in April, during our first trial, I heard the judge instruct the jury about a dozen times, telling them, in effect, that their oath bound them to a guilty verdict. Here the actors are mostly different, but the show is exactly the same—its script made up of pseudo-values and manipulations, its denouement a predictable verdict of guilt. Justice for us is a simple process: First, secure a bourgeois jury whose values coincide with those of the Establishment; then narrow the issues to black and white with no grays; exclude discussion of conscience, civil disobedience, national and international illegality; employ contempt of court to intimidate counsel; bind the jury's oath to the judge's assumption of guilt; warn that disruption of the law leads to civil anarchy, and presto—"Guilty as charged!" It's pragmatic enough to resemble technocratic war—one merely has to decide upon the end and apply the means. Any means. Justice in this case is a process of rationalizing the irrational.

Since this drama will be restaged in Milwaukee and other cities, its deeper meaning should be explored. The legal controls operative are simply the expression of the technique described above. But neither the judge, nor the two prosecutors, nor the jury sees it that way. They are convinced that they are defending the good life, the mythological probity of America, in which they have invested their emotional security. What we stand for, they cannot know, but can only fear, and hope to suppress.

We win a fight to have the film depicting the napalming shown with a soundtrack, instead of silent, as the court desires. This film has an interesting history: It has never been shown outside of court; it had been kept off the air by the local station under threat of conspiracy charges from the government. Despite requests for it from national media, despite the probability of being acquitted of conspiracy in court, the station knuckled under, thinking it safer to obey the government than to risk serving the public.

Someone told me that the film "was an exhibition of conscience that was damning for us, but redemptive to the country." It was certainly damning for us, but we were nonetheless proud of what it shows—you see us standing around the burning files, attempting to explain them to ourselves and to our countrymen. My brother says, "We did this to make it more difficult for people to kill one another." Tom Melville remarks, "These files help to provide the muscle to keep us prosperous at the expense of the world's poor." Tom Lewis explains that the napalm employed came from a recipe in the "Special Forces Handbook," and David Darst quickly adds, "We all helped to make it."

The prosecution continues by calling a Mrs. Murphy—no relation—to the stand. Mrs. Murphy is really two people—in personal life, a benign, grandmotherly Catholic lady; in government service, a narrow and doctrinaire functionary. Twenty-two years of federal propaganda and rewards have accomplished this resounding schizophrenia. On the stand, she is Mrs. Murphy, head clerk of Draft Board 33. She refers to draftees as "boys," ignoring the fact that they are men enough to kill and be killed. She testifies that we treated her with "rudeness and bad manners" (no one else recalls this), and upon question, declares that she considers working at the draft board "a service to my country," because "I am part of the army of defense."

Momentarily, the prosecution draws Mrs. Murphy's attention to neat cardboard coffins containing the ashes of her draft files. "Ruined, all ruined!" she laments. Despite her sorrow, that useless powder so carefully preserved as evi-

dence to convict us will prevent a few aluminum coffins
from coming home, and keep a few more innocent Vietnamese alive.

Under cross-examination, Mrs. Murphy is asked if she
maintained the files of men killed in Viet Nam, the Dominican Republic, Thailand, etc. She looks startled and a
bit incredulous. "Why, of course," she explains. From "greet-
ings" to epitaph, the records are cared for. "Faithfully yours
from Selective Service: I-A, GI, and *in memoriam!*"

The prosecution drones on, presenting other functionaries
as witnesses, and finally our defense begins. Bishop James
Pike, Marvin Gettleman, and Gordon Zahn come forward
to record what they would say if allowed to say it on the
stand and before a jury. (Allowed to do neither, their testimony is included in the court record.) Gordon Zahn, a
superb Christian and dear friend, says that were he allowed,
he would explain the social control of the Church by Nazism,
and the dangerous parallel presently at work in this country.
He would tell the story of a rebel and "social deviant," Franz
Jagerstatter, an Austrian peasant, who refused induction
into Hitler's army, an act of disobedience for which he was
executed. Christians must be social deviants, it seems, at
least during the time before the Parousia.

Brother David Darst is the first of the Nine to testify, beginning with a stunning account of his Christian background
and evolution. His rich and varied history made clear that
it was his whole life experience that had brought him to
Catonsville, and because the experience of the rest of us
agreed with his, it was there that our lives meshed. In the most
comprehensive way, that draft room and parking lot at
Catonsville brought meaning from the past: service in the
ghetto; militancy for civil rights and peace; conflict with
both church and state; threats to reputation, freedom, and
life itself; lecturing, writing, demonstrating, nonviolent disobedience; slow growth in the Gospel. A convergence of

priests and laymen, of hope and love, until, "so help us God," we could do nothing else but come together as one body and act.

Wednesday, October 9

Every morning before Judge Thomsen enters, our seven friends give Tom and me a briefing on events on the street. It is impossible to explain what such support means to us. Yesterday a large and joyous contingent delivered a coffin symbolizing the American war dead to the Customs House, where Tom and I poured blood last October. Last night another astonishing teach-in at St. Ignatius' Hall, where Jesuits harried by hostile parishoners hold open court for us and where thirty draft cards are burned by young men during the four-day trial.

Harold Buchman calls me to the stand at the beginning of a long and momentous day. It is fruitless to review now what I said—it is simply not worth the effort. The government outmaneuvers me. In April they had let me say what I pleased, hoping I would hang myself. When I didn't, they tried to hang me in cross-examination, both judge and jury taking turns. But that failed also.

This time, the prosecution harasses me with incessant objections to what I say about my background and experience. Harold gets into the fray, which speedily degenerates into a three-ring legal circus, with lawyers bouncing me about like balls among trained seals. I play their game by not adjusting my tactics to their challenge and by not *thinking*—an unforgivable sin in such a situation.

I step down from the stand furious with my lawyer, the prosecutors, and myself. The helplessness I feel is the only constructive element to be salvaged, because very often one wants so badly to contribute something that the process becomes an exercise in egoism. Yet, there is a lesson for resisters who come into court: Prepare your testimony well, and insist upon telling it calmly and forcefully, with no worry about contempt charges. And, in certain circumstances, keep lawyers out of the way.

George Mische and Tom Melville fight to speak their minds, thereby breaking ground for others. I found the tension during Mische's bold statements almost unbearable, as the district attorney fell back temporarily baffled. They simply do not know what to do with him and end up by letting him speak. He and Melville present a strong indictment of national policy and try to explain how men of goodwill—including those enforcing the law—are being co-opted by the system. Mary Moylan, Tom Lewis, John Hogan, and Marjorie Melville follow with their own statements—short, incisive, loving, and morally unanswerable. What can any prosecution do with people who combine joy, compassion, and keen political radicalism?

Finally, my brother Dan's turn came. Harrop Freeman questions Dan, and makes the mistake of interrupting him too often, and keeping him on the stand too long; nevertheless, Dan makes a typically brilliant impression. Of all of us, his credentials are the most impressive—a first-rate theologian, poet, and activist, he is the author of ten books and a keen student of national and international relations, perhaps the most justly celebrated priest in the country. (I know I am prejudiced, but also have the advantage of twenty years observation of his influence on high and low.)

Perhaps better than any of us, he understands that the fearful ironies of the Gospel have today converged—as I suppose they always have—with historical and political insight. So that, in the most astonishing manner, obedience to the Gospel, duty toward history, and rational politics lead together to crucifixion—whether imprisonment or death.

Dan doesn't claim any special leadership role; besides, we don't speak of leaders among the Nine—all of us have endured too many ersatz leaders to be particularly interested in the role ourselves. We are interested in meeting human need, which invariably means withstanding human injustice. These interests bind us together, and interests form a community.

Thursday, October 10

We go to court with federal marshals for the last time in this trial. A verdict is nearly certain today. Tom and I pace the marshals' cage in the Post Office Building waiting to be led handcuffed to the courtroom. The verdict, already assured, is insignificant, but some tactic must be adopted to capitalize on initiatives seized yesterday—some experiment tried in order to expose the court's pretensions of justice, and hold it morally accountable for its failure. In a word, we want to leave behind one clear and final action as a kind of legacy—bearing witness that what we did was both reasonable and obligatory. That awareness provides us with enough defense, even against courtroom procedures, even against the overkill of federal marshals.

Finally, we go to court. (We learn later that the delay was caused by a debate in the judge's chambers over the latitude to be allowed to Bill Kunstler's closing statement to the jury.)

Mr. Murphy addresses the jury with a predictable but tolerably short summary of the government's case. Kunstler again tempts the judge's wrath and gets away with it. He stresses our obedience to a higher law, and the obligation we felt to prevent further killing by an act of civil disobedience.

Mr. Skolnik, the other prosecutor, replies with an argument that I had not heard since the first trial. We possessed, he said, a "frightening arrogance" in forcing our views on other people. Nothing justifies breaking the law, no matter how hard one has tried—and failed—to make his views known through legal means. Nothing justifies turning to violence as we did; our decision was only an expression of moral and political righteousness. Skolnik is clearly more interested in our arrogance than in evidence of wanton death and destruction.

We go to lunch and immediately plunge into an intense discussion of possibilities for the afternoon. Everyone agrees that we should speak to the court, but this leaves many questions hanging. Should we seek the judge's permission or not? Should we speak before the jury leaves to deliberate? Someone observes that any attempt to speak without permission will have the marshals down on us like avenging angels. Bill Kunstler suggests that we might get permission to address the court, but not with the jury present.

Some argue for disrupting the courtroom by speaking without permission and with the jury present. But the majority say no—that would destroy the tiny chance of acquittal, a legal victory that would have incalculable value for the peace movement. It would also destroy the opportunity for dignified communication. Therefore, our lawyers will ask Judge Thomsen's permission to hear us after the jury departs.

Back in court, the atmosphere is enlivened with a doubled force of federal marshals. The story quickly gets around that the marshal guarding Tom and me at lunch had informed his chief that we were preparing for civil disobedience.

Judge Thomsen goes into an interminable instruction of the jury. (Can anyone, I reflect, retain objectivity without actively resisting what the judge is saying? Or most of it?) He offers them a contradiction for solution: Judge us according to the law, he says, and judge us according to the full range of evidence. But do it in such a way that guilt is decided, while sincerity is merely acknowledged. Then he sends them about their business.

Our lawyers come forward to present a series of motions previously denied—motions for continuance, dismissal of charges, irrelevance of indictment, restriction of intent, etc. Judge Thomsen deals with each one patiently and at length, ending a commentary on each with a flat denial.

Tom Melville has consented to act as spokesman; he rises to address the court, and we rise with him. With characteristic firmness and gentleness, Tom tells the judge that we have no confidence in a jury so chosen and instructed; would his Honor please dismiss them and sentence us himself? Judge Thomsen's answer is long and conciliatory; a guilty verdict is by no means certain, he says soothingly; let's wait and see. In turn, I have a problem for the bench, declaring that Tom and I have already been sentenced for Catonsville, so what's the point of conviction and sentence for us? He fields that one neatly, telling us that consideration will be granted us at sentencing. My brother asserts that, in effect, the court expects us to separate flesh and spirit—to bring our bodies in for sentencing, divorced from our feelings and convictions. The judge admits that he cannot match Dan's "poetic language," but that none of us seems to understand the "limitations of the court," and the fact that he (Judge Thomsen), has a "job." George Mische breaks in, then Tom Lewis, then Mary Moylan, then Dan again, then I. Each of our difficulties is handed mildly, but ineffectually. Judge Thomsen has no answers for any of us, but he makes palpable efforts to listen and to sympathize. Which is about all he can do, since he cannot very well attack the wedding between law and order. He is not even aware of the illegitimacy of the contract.

Another inspiration prevails. Tom Lewis whispers to Marjorie Melville, "What do you think of saying the Our

Father?" Marge passes the word along, and Dan rises to make the request. Judge Thomsen refers the matter to District Attorney Sachs, who walks forward and remarks, "The government has no objections, and rather welcomes the idea."

Whereupon, everyone in the courtroom—judge, prosecution, counsel, defendants, our friends—stand up to thunder out the Lord's Prayer. As *The New York Times* remarked, "The extraordinary incident was representative of the schizophrenia besetting many people—lawyers, laymen, even judges—over the question of civil disobedience to the war in Viet Nam." (October 13, 1968.)

The jury files in again, their faces as impassive and inscrutable as before. The clerk questions their foreman on the verdict: "How find you?" "Guilty," comes the answer. We hear that expected word twenty-seven times, once for each of three charges, and for nine defendants. "Beautiful!" I mutter. "It couldn't do better."

A clear voice rings out from among the spectators, "Jesus Christ has just been found guilty!"

"Take that man out," orders the judge.

"We agree," exclaim several people.

"Clear the court," orders the judge.

The court is duly cleared, many people openly sobbing. The jury, white-faced and stumbling, departs under a shield of federal marshals. When quiet is restored, the strains of "We Shall Overcome" penetrate faintly from the corridor. With only marshals and the press remaining, Dan rises to thank the judge and prosecution. We are grateful for minor or major history, whichever time decides it to be.

What did this trial mean to me? Many have asked this since. It is not easy to say; perhaps a lot of things are not yet fully understood. Many experiences in life have to be caught up with later. They often catch one unprepared because they arrive too speedily and incoherently to be grasped.

That trial meant hope to me. Hope because none of us was prey to any illusions about the verdict. We understood that we would be convicted, and we understood why. And that's a great "freedom." In contrast, the court, supposedly an instrument offering redress to free men, chose slavery to bureaucratic injustice and pollution for the Christian springs of its law. Men, while we resisted its procedures, congratulated one another on our guilt, prayed the Lord's Prayer, and thanked the court for its courtesy.

Someone has said that freedom is a state of mind. And someone at Allenwood greets newly arrived draft resisters with this remark, "They can pen up your body, but they can't have your mind. Unless you give it to them." He is an extraordinary man, a political prisoner like ourselves.

Again, that trial meant hope because of people. It's a very unchristian thing to lose hope in people; indeed, it's as bad as losing hope in God. But the fact is, since last October, we were frequently tempted to lose hope in people. With literally no help from the movement, with general neglect from the press, with official disgrace from the Church, with only a tiny circle of relatives and friends supporting us, we felt as lonely as Roland at the pass.

We forgot that we had to have time, and that people have to have time. They have to have their Chicagos, their LBJs, their Agnews, and their LeMays. You'll recall the profound confidence that men like Jefferson and Lincoln invested in people—confidence that was always verified. Americans have been brutalized by affluence, by racism and war, and by the devious machinations of empire. But they are, nonetheless, a great people. Other men seem to understand this. One bright African said recently, "You make us want to vomit more often than not. But we're stuck with you—hu-manity will live or cease to live, depending on the choices that you Americans make."

Yes, that trial meant hope—more hope than we need and more than we can use. Mary Moylan admitted on the stand that her reason for Catonsville was her desire "to celebrate life." And John Hogan said that it was to illustrate that "people have a right to be left alone." Both those great people were really talking about truth and love and justice. That is to say, about life.

October 22

Perhaps I ought to pontificate less and concentrate more on giving simple information, for mere purposes of continuity. Both Tom and I read a good deal, we "rap" with cellmates, or more commonly, listen. And I write every day, while Tom paints.

Our lawyers have again moved on appealing bail, with the usual lack of success. Now they will approach the Supreme Court again; not Chief Justice Warren this time, but Black or Douglas, who are more liberal about bail. We try to remain neutral; there are powerful arguments for accepting bail, and other good arguments for remaining in jail; in any case, the affair is entirely out of our hands, which is a good place for it to be. One might call it creative helplessness.

A letter from Dan to answer—he is back at Cornell until November 8, when we gather again for sentencing. As usual, he writes in the small hours, after a terribly hectic day. He is a man of consideration, making extraordinary efforts to inform us about our far-ranging band of activists. I sense his distress, never mentioned openly, about limited news from

us. There is a simple explanation: We are not above taking
our dearest friends for granted.

Letters are a life line, in and out of jail; very often they
are the only visible link we have with friends. Yet, how
fragile a contact they are, how vulnerable to callousness and
misunderstanding. Especially when people are trying to deal
with life, and to forestall death.

A smiling lad of fifteen drops off our laundry at the cellblock door. He is a middle-class Catholic who talked to me
soon after his arrival here. The guards have him up the hall
in a solitary cell and let him out periodically to sweep and
do errands. He works hard at being a model prisoner, hoping
for transfer from his cell and into a dormitory with the
big boys, who fascinate him. The charge against him?
Murdering his stepmother with a kitchen knife.

If one can believe him, he did not particularly dislike
her; there was no history of quarrels between them. I stood
by one day while one of the guards attempted to get a
natural response from him. "Do you know why you did
this?" His answer was a whimsical shrug of his shoulders,
followed by a prompt question about being moved from
his cell. He had apparently banished this personal horror
from his memory, deciding that it should no longer interest
him.

What is my generation doing to its young people? It is not
so much, I think, that we are malevolent or utterly lacking
in goodwill. But we have given our fiat to a social system
that is inhuman, while the kids have not. Some are strong
enough to resist the ogre (as they call it); others are hurt
so irreparably that sooner or later they lash out wildly at
the closest culprit.

More often than not, their retaliation is merciful rather
than violent. There is a young GI here who robbed three
times at gunpoint (unloaded) while waiting at a nearby

military base for his eighteenth birthday and shipment to Viet Nam. He's not clear about his motivation, except that he didn't want the money. Twice he gave it to poor families; another time, he spent it on his buddies.

October 24

This morning I answered a letter from the fiancée of a friend. By January they will be married. What makes their situation notable is that she is a divorcée and he is a priest.

I sense that they approach me hesitantly, fearing that I may add my discreet objections to those of relatives and friends. Moreover, he tends to apologize, no doubt because he contrasts my jailhouse celibacy with his better prospects.

They can spare themselves anxiety, since I have little desire to judge or envy them. I am merely concerned that they grow in freedom by marrying. If that be their fundamental intent, they have my congratulations and gratitude.

What heartens me most about the news is his intention to remain a priest. He feels that this is the best way to defend his right to marry, to help other priests faced with the same perplexity, and to challenge the widespread presumption that celibacy is something like an eighth sacrament.

Rather than risk adding an additional weight to their burdens, I spar with them charitably through the mails. His case, however, is typical enough to inspire questions for other colleagues—questions about Christian freedom and responsibility.

Most priests marry for therapeutic reasons—they seek a wife as others seek a psychiatrist. That is to say, the central problem is not sexuality as such; it is their despair of self-respect within the rigid standardization of an autocratic Church. They seize the freedom denied them to realize their ideals, not to claim identity within the Church, but to form a new life, and supposedly, a new freedom.

And so they leave, marry, but almost always move into another bureaucracy—to do a compromised job in education, publishing, or antipoverty work. Their overall condition, in human or Christian terms, seldom improves, and frequently worsens. Their former dependence upon the authority of superiors, respect from the laity, and a stereotyped service is transferred to a new setting—but one in many ways very similar. They exchange one kind of control for another—along with the added responsibility for board and the added privilege of bed.

I have a question, therefore, for those priests who would leave to marry, or merely get married. What is the state of your freedom? Or, perhaps it would be better to phrase it: Whom are you serving now? (Many priests, of course, will have been too deeply scored by their experience to find time for such questions; others, however, will give them courageous attention.)

Scores of priests I knew have married, but of them all, only one seems to have done so in freedom, to become thereby a better man, a better priest. His wife shared his grasp of the real, loving as profoundly as himself the people they served. Their future is already in jeopardy, with a certainty of separation and prison, and with a possibility of death not far removed. They accept this future with magnificent calm, since they have chosen it as they have chosen each other, and because it allows them to possess each other in an entirely superior way. They were married to man before marrying each other, and even as the first marriage caused the second, so the second has enriched the first. He puts it this way, "My marriage has made me a better man and a better priest."

One of the more abused phrases in Saint Paul—"It remaineth, that both they that have wives be as though they had none" (I Corinthians 7:29)—must be seen today in a broader and more worthy light. It would dishonor the Apostle to imply that he spoke only of sexual abstinence. Rather, his concern was for the freedom necessary to preach the Gospel. This freedom remains a necessity to which Christians must subject their marriages. Truth, charity, and justice have always required that the needs of the human family have as much claim on us as the needs of our own kin—with as great a call on our service.

This is the freedom I would wish for my friend in his marriage.

October 27

Less than ten days to election. We have an idea in the informal diplomatic hopper which may have possibilities for peace. It depends now on who else agrees, especially the North Vietnamese.

After the last release of captured fliers to American peace people—subsequent to the one involving my brother Dan and Howard Zinn last February—Tom Lewis thought of an interesting refinement for the next release. Why not present Washington with a dilemma: "No more American fliers released except to antiwar people presently in U.S. jails?"

We have mulled over some of the delicious ramifications of such a proposal, its benefit to the Vietnamese, and its apparent liability but actual benefit to the United States as well.

Benefit to the Vietnamese: The fliers are war criminals, more responsible for scorched earth and civilian massacre than any other element of our ruthless, technological war machine in Viet Nam. To put it bluntly, they are major actors of genocide. Despite their mindless atrocities, the North Vietnamese have treated them in strict conformity to the Geneva Convention, protecting them from enraged peasants and giving them adequate medical care, food, and clothing. To free them is to belie the assumption that the corruption of total war strikes both sides equally. To give them their liberty against all right and expectation is, finally, to score a brilliant moral and propaganda victory.

Apparent liability, actual benefit to Washington: Our proposal, we think, presents the United States Government with a classic dilemma of impotent power. If, on the one hand, it rejects conditions set by the North Vietnamese for freeing the fliers, it could face a resounding public outcry that might be difficult to manipulate to any political advantage. If, on the other hand, it accepts the conditions, it admits that the return of the fliers depends entirely upon those serious enough in their "nay-saying" to end up in its jails. In a word, Washington might be forced to admit, however grudgingly or implicitly, that its "enemies" are in reality its best friends.

Obviously, Washington wants its fliers back. They are the problem in a problematic situation. Their training and indoctrination have been expensive, their losses so heavy that pilot shortages have sometimes embarrassed strike capacities, their release a sure source of partisan political benefit, and their presence in North Vietnamese prison camps an added weight to the documentations of the War Crimes Tribunal.

In any event, we conveyed Tom's idea to Dan, who suggested further variations. First, amnesty for the political prisoners sent to receive the captured fliers; or, second, a broader program of *quid pro quo* that could apply to the future—freedom for amnesty, one pilot for one imprisoned resister.

Though Dan had met in Hanoi a leading member of the North Vietnamese delegation in Paris, he nonetheless thought it best to work through David Dellinger or Tom Hayden of the National Mobilization Committee. He tried repeatedly to reach them during the summer, but to no avail. Of course, they had ample excuses, because of their preparations for the Democratic National Convention in Chicago.

During the trial we revived the idea again, commissioning Douglas Dowd of Cornell and Howard Zinn of Boston University to approach the North Vietnamese. They in turn endeavored to obtain Dellinger's support, since the North Vietnamese regard him as A. J. Muste's successor and unofficial head of the American Peace Movement. Dellinger finally agreed—his recommendation to Paris being complemented by a letter from Mr. Tran Van Dinh, former chargé d'affaires from Saigon to Washington. At this point, the matter now rests.

Meanwhile, Tom and I wait. As the only elderly antiwar people in prison, we seem the logical ones to go. Time slips quickly by, narrowing a unique opportunity to demonstrate the colossal threat of the war and the Johnson regime's complicity in it. If the Democrats lose next month, they will presumably avoid any action that threatens to discredit them. And as victors, the Republicans can reasonably disavow responsibility for the Viet Nam morass and seek other means to free the fliers. On the other hand, if the Democrats win, our strong bargaining position with them remains, since Humphrey will have inherited not only power from his predecessor but also debts, duplicities, and corrupt geopolitics.

We pray as best we can—for our friends around the world and for our countrymen. Tom fasted today, the anniversary of our blood pouring last October 27. Such measures appeal best to the higher powers. And they teach us patience.

October 29

"We got thirteen people in here. Like it or not, you mothers gotta live together!" Ernie, a veteran of fourteen years of jail, had just helped to break up a fight, and the rest of us, including the belligerents, were anxiously gathered to rebuild the peace. We listened respectfully to Ernie; he knew the psychology of convicts and the kind of discipline necessary for prison survival.

It all seemed like a most unlikely takeoff on the old theme of unity and diversity. Success was far more unlikely here than in Greenwich Village, where I had once heard Miles Davis convert the anger, hope, anguish, beauty, and exaltation of black existence into an all-embracing jazz. With a medium of incredible power and freedom, Davis had said that black people want to belong, but as black people. It appeared that something similar was happening now.

Let it be clear that thirteen men in a cellblock as small as this is like Tabby in her shoebox after having five kittens. Who outside would dare to pack thirteen people in a space like ours, even if the people were presumably less violent than we? Such an arrangement wouldn't even be tried in Harlem, itself so congested as to be humanly unlivable. ("Concentrate the whole national population into New York's five boroughs," the sociologists say, "and the result would be Harlem's density of people.")

Yet we get along here, better than one would have expected. We get along despite the guards' frequent habit of dumping problem prisoners on us—the young hardened types, the physical and emotional cripples. Despite all that impressive behavioral research on aggression, neurotic excitability, and ruthlessness, we get along fine for the most part.

TV helps, however superficial the unity into which it draws people. Its channels provide the jailhouse equivalent of a pacification program. Here is a substitute for the unremitting boredom, distraction from the anxious prospect of trial and sentence, a rerouting of aggression. There is rapt involvement among the prisoners during the cops-and-robbers serials—their gesticulations, running commentary, and offhand assurances that "they would have escaped" are beyond description.

More influential than TV as a unifying factor, however, is jail itself: The community of shared calamity that emerges is impressive in many respects. Analogously, militarists know from millennia of experience that, except in action, where he sees his comrades die, a soldier will rarely be a killer. In battle, death becomes a catalyst for the living; killing, a necessity and a bond. Here confinement serves the same purpose; a necessity to be borne, it forms a common bond. For most prisoners jail approaches the ultimate in adversity, a condition that both claims and evokes sympathy.

Consequently, a man can enter jail charged with the most repulsive crimes (which he may freely admit to his fellows; there is little dishonesty with one's fellows in this area) and he will still have immediate credentials for acceptance in the brotherhood. A man can come in sick, mad, foulmouthed, brutish as regards cleanliness or human consideration, and allowances will be made for him with the most remarkable charity. For he shares the common affliction— jail; the common enemy—cops and courts; and the common goal—freedom. Bars and locks have done for him what love did for the early Christians; what outrage did for Fidel and Che; what greed does for bankers and power for politicians: They have formed a community of interest.

As for diversity, we have more than our share—two black teen-agers, material witnesses to murder; two acid heads (their term, not mine) picked up by narcotics agents; six burglars and/or hustlers; two antiwar people; and Jeremiah. We represent the ghetto; the black and white communities; the middle class; the Church, small "c" or large; federal and state jails; formal and informal education; a range of arts, skills, and professions; venality, compassion, and indifference—not an ideal slice of values, but a rather remarkable sample.

Jeremiah is something else—tall, slim, black, and eighteen years old, with a twenty-five-inch waist and a light heavy-weight's shoulders. "Jeremiah's a beautiful cat," one of our friends said, paying tribute to his modesty and restraint, his readiness to listen and to help, and his quick, self-effacing grin. Even more than these qualities, however, what drew attention was Jeremiah's intangible air of tragedy, too profound to understand and too fearful to explore, a burden which he bore resolutely, never forcing it upon others in the slightest.

Even the kids noticed it. "Man, Jeremiah's got bad troubles, ain't he?" asked a black fourteen-year-old. Indeed he had. For while Jeremiah didn't have the world on his back, he did have the state of Maryland, and its charge of murdering his young wife. Because of which, guilty or not, insane or not, jailed or free, Jeremiah saw no point in living, desiring nothing so much as an opportunity to kill himself, as he openly told me one day, and as the other prisoners suspected.

In theory we know, yet we still have to learn, that a man cannot be weighed like a flounder or summed up like a column of figures. And that the limitations of a sixth-grade ghetto school education do not deprive someone of deep feeling and complexity. Which is a way of saying that despite all my pious and/or liberal clichés, my attitude toward Jeremiah was characteristically white, and my relationship that of a benign overseer, a paternalism of indifference. As long as he didn't foul up plantation routine by disturbing my reading and writing, as long as he acted as a good "hand," I could conveniently assume that he was going through regeneration, that he was becoming a good "field nigger."

But life doesn't work quite that way. Jeremiah took to sleep as an opiate, and since a healthy person can sleep only so much, he slept all day and not at night, despite the sleeping pills he begged from the guards. He began to eat poorly, to talk seldom, and to fall into bouts of fitful anger, like the shrill rages of a spoiled child. Twice he and I discussed his situation, but a combination of shame and distrust prevented him from being frank about his wife's death. Obviously he didn't care enough about what happened to him to confide fully in anyone.

In one sense, individual life is the interplay of contesting desires, values, and forces; of action and reaction; of struggling to establish the sort of "harmony of interest" that our diplomats speak about so ambiguously. Very often, human need must swell to the point of crisis before it can express itself effectively, and before others can recognize and answer it. This was apparently the situation with Jeremiah.

Ridicule, which is such a routine element of prison socialization, helped to contribute to the crisis. Under jail conditions, a man's origin, veracity, authenticity, and life style are all subjected to relentless and comical goading. This is not just indoor sport, not just a response to the fishbowl quality of prison life, but the assertion of a common humanity, and of one's desire to see others respond to a test. "I am a man" becomes, at the same time, a challenge to others: "If you're a man, prove it."

Needless to say, Jeremiah was disadvantaged in this kind of battle, having little interest in proving himself or testing others. More than anything, he wanted, desperately, to be left alone. Unfortunately, one of our more energetic moralists began to ridicule him one evening, and after a few quiet warnings were unavailing, Jeremiah exploded on his tormentor with an awesome display of pure fury. It took several of us to pull him off, and had we not intervened, the affair would have ended in serious injury, or even death.

Minutes later, Jeremiah came over to talk, sobbing inconsolably. He knew that I had seen his rage; now I was seeing his tears. What it cost him to transcend his shame, no one will ever know. The encounter with his tormentor had proved to him again that he was a mystery to himself, and a very violent one. It also reminded him that the devastating rage he had just shown had also been responsible for his wife's death.

Jeremiah told me of his fears, and of the torture they brought him. He did not fear life, or other people, or the future as such, but only in the light of his capacity to erupt and destroy when given the provocation. He was terribly afraid of himself, and had no will to live, because living might mean killing at any time.

What does hope mean for him? A society that is violent to its core can make few provisions for those who are victims of its lessons. Jeremiah has a long shot at an insanity plea, putting himself at the mercy of our pitifully understaffed and ineffectual mental institutions. If that fails, he will languish in a state penitentiary, a casualty of the Great Society.

The "acid heads" remark that life has been a bum trip for Jeremiah. And one of our more jocular burglars, not distinguished for his love of blacks, comments that life has dealt Jeremiah "low cards in spades." All I know is that despite his remarkable gifts of life, death haunts his waking hours and disturbs his sleep. If anything, I suspect that Jeremiah was guilty of loving his wife too much, of placing impossible demands upon her. When she failed him, he failed himself—and killed her.

In any case, he needs hope and the will to live and the conviction that what he endures now is the price of being a man. God has given Jeremiah a full cup of suffering. May He also send him friends, steadfast and compassionate. Starting with those who are with him in prison. Only with friends can a man have hope in this sacred adventure we call life.

STATEMENT AT SENTENCING, NOVEMBER 8, 1968

Judge Thomsen, Mr. Murphy, Mr. Skolnik, members of the jury, dear friends. This last month in Baltimore County Jail has given Tom Lewis and myself ample time to reflect on our trial. We have tried to avoid a simplistic view which would reduce it to mere questions of innocence or guilt, acquittal or conviction. Nor do we care to reduce this occasion to one of light or heavy sentence. Rather, we desire to communicate with the bench, with the prosecution, and our country. The rest is incidental.

We owe Judge Thomsen gratitude for his willingness to listen, and to give our objections sympathetic consideration. Indeed, we conversed with him more as a friend than as a judge. We owe Mr. Murphy and Mr. Skolnik gratitude because their prosecution never departed from dignity, never stooped to derision or vindictiveness. We regard them also as friends.

We feel that this day will continue the honest and restrained discourse of our trial. Though disagreements will remain profound, no disparagement or bitterness will interfere from either side. As free men, we will talk about mutual responsibilities to mankind, and to this nation. My part in the conversation follows.

A visitor at the jail remarked to us last week, "President Johnson has undercut you people again [the last time being in March]. Like the court, his bombing halt says that only due process is effective for peace. He's telling you there's no need to break the law. Maybe you ought to leave politics out of your statements on Friday."

Our friend was downcast that our position had eroded so abruptly. What a dilemma. He seemed to be saying, no position, and all those consequences. But of course, we cannot agree. Rather we see the bombing halt as another instance of carrot-and-stick diplomacy. In other words, the President dangles the carrot by stopping the bombing, and swings the stick by escalating the war. He engineers an enormously publicized concession and nullifies it immediately by quiet countermeasures.

Regarding the war in the South, an American military source said this: "There's going to be relentless, continuing pressure on all fronts. This includes the big battalion war, pacification, and elimination of the enemy infrastructure." (*Baltimore Morning Sun*, Nov. 4, 1968.) Naval and air armadas previously bombarding the North have now joined their massive counterparts in the South, bombing supply lines, arms depots, and troop concentrations. In the Mekong Delta area, our river fleets have started Operation Sea Lords, an unprecedented attempt to clear the rivers of enemy supply traffic. Meanwhile, our military blandly admits that the North Vietnamese have withdrawn considerable portions of their troops; that there has been no shelling over the DMZ into our positions, and that general de-escalation seems to be an enemy rule. Meanwhile, the President makes it clear that if the enemy responds to "our relentless, continuing pressure," if the enemy attacks our bases or the larger cities, General Abrams may—at his discretion—take necessary measures, including resumption of the bombing.

In fact, very little has changed. While one must gratefully admit that the bombing must stop for negotiations to begin, one can also warn against the conference table being used as a smokescreen under which the killing continues. In such an event, the bloody duplicity of the battlefield is faithfully repeated in Paris—under Robert's Rules of Order.

What has the bombing halt accomplished? Thank God, it has removed our sky-borne terrorists from the skies of North Viet Nam. But it has also shifted domestic and world opinion in our favor; it has placed responsibility for continuing the war on the Vietnamese, and it has given us precious time to pursue the National Liberation Front, which is the main adversary in the war. In effect, the bombing halt and negotiations, even with the Front, cost us nothing. They can continue indefinitely, until we force them on the battlefield. And gain a Korean-type solution.

Therefore, our position remains unchanged, despite the feeling of some that we no longer have one. The United States has nothing to negotiate with the Vietnamese except unconditional withdrawal, and indemnities owed for genocide and ecological destruction. (As if these can be paid for.) We can, as well, arrange for the safety of our South Vietnamese mercenaries. Many of them will not need help; they will merely follow their loot to Hong Kong and Switzerland.

Moreover, I think that we have made it clear that our dissent runs counter to more than the Viet Nam war, which is but one manner in which American power acts itself. It also acts itself in concentrating wealth, and in creating poverty. In 1900 America had three thousand millionaires; in

1960 it had twenty-seven thousand; today it has perhaps thirty thousand. One percent of our families own eighty percent of all individually held corporate stocks, and twenty-eight percent of the nation's entire personal wealth. At the bottom of the dollar pyramid, one-third of our people, or sixty-five million strong, own one percent of the national wealth. (Daniel Friedenberg, *The Radical Papers; A Fabian Program for America*, Doubleday Anchor Books.) Of these sixty-five million, forty million are poor and ten million are literally starving. (*Hunger, USA;* 100-page report presented to Congress by Citizens' Board of Inquiry into Hunger and Malnutrition in the U.S.; April 22, 1968. Also, the CBS report *Hunger, USA;* May 21, 1968.) As the record shows, being an American in more than name is a highly selective —and economic—process.

Judging from their callousness toward American poverty, our men of power take an implicit pride in the fact that only one-fifth of our people are poor, while three-fourths of the world's people are poor. Whatever the case, they preserve the permanence of "have–have—not" gaps by 112 billion in overseas investments, an indispensable factor in American control of the world's finance and business. Such ambitious frontiersmanship demands of course the vigilance supplied by history's most powerful military establishment, which is a twofold blessing in our midst. Depending on one's point of view, it keeps the peace and/or protects our investments; and it injects an annual eighty billion into the economy. In a word, our military gives new meaning to the old Gospel prophecy: "I tell you that everyone that has will be given more; but from him who does not have much, that which he has will be taken away." (Luke 19:26.)

Such has been our side of a dialogue with power for years. On power's side, we have met little understanding, much silence, much suspicion, much scorn and punishment. Nobody—I repeat, nobody—does "their thing" like power, because nobody is so intent upon survival and more power. Mr. Skolnik spoke of the "fantastic arrogance" which led us to Catonsville, because, as he said, "they couldn't convince enough people quickly enough of their point of view." Perhaps. But to even the scales I would like him to speak publicly of the "fantastic arrogance" of our leaders, and their crimes against the Vietnamese and the American poor. This much Mr. Skolnik must admit: No court will try them, no jail will receive them, and few will dare to call them "arrogant."

We wonder if Acton's saying applies here: "Power corrupts, and absolute power corrupts absolutely." Or John Kennedy's words: "Those who deny peaceful revolution are most responsible for violent revolution."

We have but one message for our leaders, in whose manicured hands the power of this land lies. Lead us! Lead us by giving people justice, and there will be no need to break the law, no need for civil disobedience. Let President Nixon do what his predecessor failed to do—let him obey the rich less and the people more; let him think less of the privileged and more of the poor; less of America and more of the world. Let our bishops and religious superiors think less of buildings and more of people; less of casuistry and more of the beatitudes; less of comfort and more of poverty; less of authority and more of service. Let lawmakers, judges, and lawyers think less of law and more of justice; less of legal rituals and more of human rights.

Dialogue, we have found painfully, is a two-way street. As for us, we have long listened to our leaders. We are still listening today. At the end of these proceedings, and under the sanctimonious heading of the law, our leaders will speak to us by returning Tom and myself to jail. Perhaps my brother and our other friends as well. We will listen and we will accept, knowing that at the point of push and shove, our leaders speak that way. But first we have this to say. To the new administration we say that war, racism, and greed are now institutionalized in this society, as the Defense budget, the Kerner Report, and the Gross National Product prove.

The norms of justice and democratic representation must be applied to these colossal injustices, or America will be torn from within and assaulted from without. To our bishops and superiors we say: Learn something about the Gospel and about illegitimate power. When you do, you will liquidate investments, take a house in the slums, or even join us in jail. We know that many of you belong there, but we would like to hear *you* say it. To lawyers we say: Defend draft resisters for nothing, as our lawyers have defended us; insist on justice for them; risk contempt of court if necessary, and go to jail with your clients. To the prosecution we say: Refuse to indict and to try opponents of the war, and prefer resignation and private practice to doing so. To federal judges we say: Give antiwar people suspended sentences to work for justice and peace, or resign. As Martin Luther King would say, I have a dream: Federal judges, district attorneys, and marshals against the war in Viet Nam.

Our leaders have told us that the Establishment is reformable. Let them reform it, then, and we will help with all our conviction and energy. In jail or out. Thank you.

PRISON JOURNAL, CONTINUED

November 9, 1968

Let's suppose that, journalistically speaking, it were the best of possible worlds. Let's suppose that a reporter wheedled his way into this jail to get an interview—a rare reporter, one gifted with humanity, brains and guts. In that order. Let's suppose his newspaper was free of debts, notes and mortgages—economic and political—and therefore, was ideologically free as well.

With such a reporter, and for such a paper, let's imagine the following interview:

Reporter. How do you feel about being interviewed in jail?
Berrigan. I'm surprised at the way you got in here. Being in jail might lend a little more conviction to what I say. Not lucidity necessarily, but conviction.

I seem to recall that last May, Time Magazine *called your brother and you the most revolutionary priests in the coun-*

try. How did they mean that—as a compliment, or as a calculation of the Catholic Church's neutrality? I'm suspicious about Time, *with its ambiguity.*

In other words, are we guys good in our own right, or do we look good because we come from nothing?

That's right. A lot of people are asking the question, and there are others more important. Let's go on. *Time* may be ambiguous to you, but it isn't regarding national interest— it's for motherhood, flag and Gross National Product. And it would be the last journal to indict the Church's neutrality— too much sympathy of interest. So it would be an unusual *Time* reporter who would understand what kind of revolution Dan and I stand for.

What kind do you stand for?

You're nothing if not direct. We try to stand for the kind taught and lived by Christ, which is a revolution of a person through truth and love. We try to say as he did that Christ in man (truth and love) is the main revolutionary force in the world, capable of changing even American institutions. We try to make these beliefs articles of faith, even facts, if you will. With most revolutionaries they tend to be curiosities, or assumptions. Mostly because of the horrid example of Christians. In a word, we try.

Somebody once said that priests never entirely break through abstract thinking. They learn their theology so well, they never learn to talk about it concretely. Is what you just said an example of this?

No. Maybe it was a reaction to your question, which wasn't quite fair. Interviews have their limitations, and one of them is limit. You seem to want a summary of belief and life in two short sentences. Then too, concrete expression doesn't eliminate the need for abstraction. It heightens it, if anything.

Sorry. You were telling about the kind of revolution the

Berrigans stand for. I find it hard to connect what you've said with breaking into draft boards and destroying records.
Not just the Berrigans, but more and more Christians, orthodox and unorthodox. We say that Christ requires us to affirm life, to insist on its dignity and sacredness, and to oppose its abuse and destruction. Christ requires us to affirm his sovereignty over man, a sovereignty of justice, peace and freedom. Now, all this is revolution, but of a terribly positive kind. Standing for life means just that, including standing against any threat to life.

Let me understand you. Are you implying that human weakness expresses itself mostly by domination, or by control through exploitation and naked force? And that resistance to this is revolution?
Nonviolent resistance to domination is revolution. I severely question the worth of violent revolution, because it doesn't attack the fundamental problem, which is what we call sin, man's tendency to dominate man. The students use a phrase: "A revolution is always as violent as the violence it combats." I find that fatalistic, vague and very dangerous, because it suggests that revolution is no more than a butting of heads, with the thickest skull winning. It also suggests that a revolutionary must meet oppressors in their own jungles, and use only their own weapons. So it misses the point that revolution is first spiritual before it is political. Because that lesson has not been taught—it is a fundamental Christian lesson—we have a dilemma in which violence will most probably be the main instrument of change.

You confuse me, because I know you'd be the last person to claim that Cubans and Vietnamese have been brutalized by their revolutions.
I know it. The fact is, they haven't—I have that on very good authority. At least a partial explanation comes from the nature of their struggle: in one case, liberation from fascism; and

the other, liberation from foreign control. National defense, if you will, with violent resistance the only available human resource. (Batista was backed by the U.S.) Then too, a profound drive for social justice has in both cases tempered the effects of violence. It's a very complex question.

Despite my reservations, I'll admit that you put a twist on the revolution that I've never thought of.
Perhaps. I'm trying to say that the connotation of violence that we usually associate with revolution is a huge illusion. By it, revolutionaries talk about forcing justice, when justice just isn't forced. Christ's saying that discipleship means daily self-denial and daily acceptance of the cross is immeasurably more to the point than a romanticism like revolution coming out of the muzzle of a gun. Justice in the U.S. isn't even a priority, human brotherhood is. Simply because man is a brotherhood. And to seek that is a gain, even if the seeking cannot avoid a rending of this society piecemeal, with Americans hunting one another like mad dogs.

What are your hopes that this can be done?
That what can be done?

I'm very pragmatic. That this society can be saved from being rended piecemeal?
That depends. I believe that one man promotes human brotherhood by serving it in love and suffering. I also believe that this is the best way to save America from its crimes. Whether it will happen that way is up to God and other people. My hopes run very high, and they are not denied by the fact that our desperate need for revolution comes from the scarcity of people who can make one, in a human fashion.

That "one man" you speak of, is that you? You're the first priest in jail over a political issue in decades.

Not at all. I merely followed others. And there are others who have suffered much more than I.

I notice that this spiritual revolution you speak of has both a personal and social obligation. Why distinguish the two? Why not stress that a truly human being—a man, a Christian —must embody a whole duty toward man?

Because it seems to me that a technocracy tends to make schizophrenics of us. I know daily communicants who work in the Pentagon and at Ft. Detrick, which is, as you know, the world's center for biological-warfare research. That is so for the most part because power (economics) dictates national culture, which controls religion by a divide-and-conquer technique. That is to say, personal moraliy is encouraged because it lends stability to power, and helps power to control. Public morality, however, is discouraged generally —tolerated when it is verbal, repressed when it is illegal. That illegal public morality is repressed has a clear and definite reason—*it is the only one worthwhile.*

Let me give you an example. I'm jailed at Allenwood with a lot of young Jehovah's Witnesses. I asked one recently if their parents and friends worked in defense plants. He answered, "No, hardly ever." I asked why. He thought for a moment and then remarked, "Because we're opposed to war in any form." A beautiful explanation, right to the point, from a relatively simple kid who belonged to a very disliked sect. Yet he saw more than most Christians and, obviously, he was doing more. He told me, in effect, there's no sense in my being in jail while relatives work in defense. No moral schizophrenia in him.

Has Gandhi influenced what you have done?

I can't tell you how much. To me, he is an unorthodox Christian saint. If canonizations have any point today, this man deserves to be canonized. Rome ought to stage a spectacular for him. Undoubtedly, Christ was the central influ-

ence in his life; yet he found no contradiction between
reverence for the Gospel and rejection of institutional
Christianity. It was the Gospel which gave Gandhi compassion and his incredible confidence in voluntary suffering as
a tactical and political force. He was a lover of humanity
and, therefore, a man of God. His teaching and example have
changed even mighty America, though no American disciple
has approached his vision and courage. But we might have
some yet.

Are you referring to Martin Luther King when you say that?
King was a great man who died a great man's death. But in
my opinion, the Nobel Peace Prize sent him into decline, so
did a series of Civil Rights Bills. Once power set him up by
an illusion of progress, they could have him for dinner at
their leisure. His vision of suffering love faded, and with it,
his sense of political flexibility. Consequently, his nonviolence became so unimaginative and safe that the Establishment relaxed. They no longer had to take him seriously. He
went to Chicago, where Richard Daley emerged the victor,
not King. As for SCLC, excepting its early days, it never got
with the black poor—too much "progress" to protect, as well
as King's image. In a sense, King had plenty to learn from
Malcolm X, and he didn't learn. Whereas Malcolm learned
from King.

*If I remember correctly, Gandhi was very scrupulous about
not destroying property, while you people have made a point
of it. And yet you claim fidelity to his teaching. Where's the
contradiction?*
There isn't any that I can see. Gandhi's India bears no resem-
blance to imperial America. Americans have an attachment
to private property (public property too, since is makes private property secure) that borders on the obsessive. Property
is a Way of Life, it is the rationale behind globalism. In
India, Gandhi had a spiritual goal of brotherhood and a

political goal of independence for India. He didn't need to tamper with property to achieve these goals.

He wanted the British out; we want poor Americans in. He wanted national autonomy; we want political representation. To attain that here, one must engage the issue of private property. Draft files illustrate better than any item of private or public property—except hydrogen bombs—the savagery that Americans will use to defend private property. Draft files make it possible to fight wars cheaply—wars necessary to guard an expanding economy.

Now, that's what I call a poor job of making violence plausible. At least, you haven't convinced me. The Catonsville Nine and the Milwaukee Fourteen seized Selective Service files by force, and burned them. I might approve of what you've done, but don't call it nonviolence. That's quibbling. It depends on what kind of violence you're talking about. The most violent forces in the world are truth and love, yet they're constructive. Truth and love aim to destroy idols, you know; they separate people from illusions, and bring them into the real world.

There is no greater service. You'll recall that the Israelite prophets verbally and physically attacked idols, and Christ cleansed the temple in the same tradition.

We learned that the violence done to draft clerks at the Custom House and at Catonsville was spiritual rather than physical. Because of painful precautions, no one was hurt at the Customs House, and one woman slightly at Catonsville. But we assaulted their consciences, an unavoidable and fruitful result of ruining their precious files. Why should draft clerks be immune from moral contact—any more than guards at Buchenwald, pilots of nuclear bombers, or scientists at Ft. Detrick? They are all technicians of death machinery—or grease-monkeys, at the very least.

*But I still think that if you get violent with things, you get
violent with persons eventually. A basic part of the American
cult of violence is to rape nature, from there to graduate to
raping people like Indians, blacks, Orientals, foreigners—
anybody that's vulnerable, and whose vulnerability can turn
a profit. But this business of idols—who's to judge who has
what idols, and whether they deserve to be destroyed?*

Spoken like a true liberal. I love you. You take a flagrant
wrong—violence (waste of things by the wealthy), and turn
it into an argument against dissenters. Can't you see that the
rich abuse things indiscriminately, things which belong to
the poor? And that their hang-ups with things makes them
genteel beasts with other people? And when we attack property in order to educate the rich—to tell them that their fun
and games have people starving and dying early—you start
worrying about the state of our souls. That's a red herring.

Scripture has some violent langauge for the rich, amost never
used. "Come now, you rich," St. James says, "weep and howl
over your miseries which will come upon you." (James 5, 1).
James railed against ill-gotten gains and he was death on
staying rich while the poor stayed poor. Now, for the Jet Set
to throw million-dollar parties and stay on perpetual vacations is an obscenity that threatens man. One can no longer
call this kind of prostitution a moral lapse; one has to call it
political crime, crime against humanity.

*You seem anxious over a future for the rich. Mankind will
judge them in time, hopefully with mercy. To separate them
from their booty without harming them physically is a favor.
It is their booty, after all, which dehumanizes them.*

To go back to your first point. It's a different cry to abuse
nature for profit, or to rob people of their land and labor;
and to attack property which makes robbery attractive.
That's right, Selective Service is law and is *property making*

robbery attractive. And who makes the robbery attractive? Easy—the very people who are robbed, who pay the highest taxes and supply the blood. Our poor, our lower middle-class, our South Vietnamese mercenaries. Seventy percent of the GI's in Viet Nam are draftees; thirty percent of our combat troops are black (a statistic dutifully obscured by the Pentagon). If our troops weren't so damn cheap to us, they wouldn't be so expendable. Selective Service is such an economy operation that duplicate records aren't kept, while the clerks receive only fair plantation wages. Then there's the scandal of military pay for our fighting men. That is to say, if we had to pay a volunteer army to protect our overseas investments, we wouldn't sacrifice that army so readily. And maybe we'd be more cautious about overseas investments. That's the name of the game, you know; that's what war is all about. Who's going to control the profits?

So I think it's a glaring inversion of values to agonize over the moral consternation we cause in draft boards, while ignoring the fact that draft machinery ends in murder. Somewhere the making the connection between induction and burning Vietnamese children, the American imagination breaks down, because it prefers not to believe that, alongside us, the Nazis were simply crude, Goebbels could learn lessons from Johnson, and there's no comparison between the *blitzkrieg* and total war against ecology, the helpless, even the unborn. Except that we have preserved our "innocence," while the Nazis didn't pretend they had any.

Oh, come on now. I can understand opposition to nasty war, but let's not get irrational about it. The fact is, we're not Nazis, or anything like them.

We'll get nowhere arguing it. I heard a famous American correspondent—a Jew—and the former ambassador from Saigon to the U.S. go round and round on this question. It was the Vietnamese who compared us to the Nazis and I tended to agree with him though I had seen some of the crematoria, and the residue taken from them. But they got nowhere, just as you and I are getting nowhere. I'm just saying that in Viet Nam, our military technology takes the blame for one of the most atrocious wars in history. To the Vietnamese, genocide is a fact, but most of our fighting men remain morally unscathed. Only the dogfaces (infantry) see their handiwork, but propaganda has given them a vision of little brown people swarming up the California beaches. The flyboys are different—they cut in the afterburners, push bomb-releases, sweat out the flack and tail it for home. B-52 crewmen push bomb releases and sweat out nothing—they are insulated by 50,000 feet. They see aerial photographs later, but they never see people blown to bits or buried alive, or animals slaughtered, or earth torn asunder. By the time the bombs hit, they're returning to Guam or Thailand and admiring the sunset. And so they sleep nights, and wait contentedly for the next mission. And a chaplain's blessing for bombs-on-target.

Let's get on to something else. Let's talk about the revolution that beckons in the U.S. Or so many people think. Is it possible to chart any of its lines?
Nobody knows much about revolution in an affluent society. There's never been one. However, I think that one ought to speculate about it, about signs of the times and how they are apt to develop. There's a multitude of intangibles, and of presently unanswerable questions. Here's one. How can a revolution grow when the workers are not the poor, and therefore, content when the poor are unorganized, and when the workers are organized against the poor?

I don't know—you're answering the questions. The workers do seem firmly wedded to management—they want business as usual. But with that a fact, and with the vast intelligence and police resources of government, how can an uprising start?

I don't know that, either. I do know that most Americans are bewildered and fearful; that leadership is astonishingly mediocre; that large numbers of students, blacks, GI's, poor and intellectuals are alienated; and that our ruthless experiments in racism and cold war are beginning to pay us back in counterfeit coin. We are the only nation on earth that could survive three centuries of racism, a hundred years of Open Door and twenty years of cold war. But not for much longer, or so it seems.

Prime Minister Trudeau of Canada said in November, 1968, that he expected the U.S. to be in civil war in six years. Coming from the head of a satellite state, it is a surprising statement, and—perhaps—an accurate one. Despite available repressive power, social breakup seems slowly to escalate, retarded mainly by a fearful and defensive middle class. Obviously, if it comes, it will not repeat the sectional struggle of our Civil War. More likely, it will be ideological. On the one side, there will be those rebeling against neo-capitaist corruption and technocratic control—those generally favoring a socialist democracy. On the other, there will be those willing to accept stronger elements of fascism to assure police protection, repression of blacks, lower taxes, continuing prosperity and firm anti-communism. Not surprisingly, the struggle will revolve around radically different views toward private property.

Let me say this. Your views seem striking for their pessimism, and for their lack of historical perspective. This country has had internal difficulties before—everything from the Chicago Massacre to the Civil Rights era—and it's always adjusted, always found the redress. Maybe you're creating a self-fulfilling prophecy here; if enough people say this country's going to blow up, it will.

Oh, oh—you're flashing your liberal credentials again. It's
true we've adjusted to internal strife, but always by a more
energetic push overseas. You'll recall Gandhi's famous phrase
about means containing their ends. Either you don't see the
kind of financial adventurism we're doing overseas, or you're
trying to create discussion. Let's suppose the first. In 1946,
at the end of World War II, we had $8,000,000,000 in over-
seas investments; now we have $140,000,000,000. Why the
race overseas? Because the profits are there—in Labrador, in
the Andes, in the Middle East, in Indochina, and soon in
Austria and Yugoslavia, which Rusk just annexed to NATO
(informally for now). Not in the slums nor in Appalachia
nor in rural Mississippi, nor in our polluted air and rivers, nor
in new schools, hospitals and community centers. In the last
analysis, you see, free enterprise isn't "free" at all. It has a
determinism which impels it to *profits* before people, *death*
before life. Detroit is the best example at hand. It has a
greedy hand in killing fifty thousand of us a year, and strangling the rest with toxic air!
Sooner or later, people will rebel against such camoflaged
ruin, with its addenda of nuclear overkill, genocide in Viet
Nam and official lies. Let me anticipate another objection by
saying that rigidity and irreformability come from the system, not from the people who say it *must* be otherwise.
Spare me a moment of arrogance—a six-year sentence in a
federal pen (it could have been more) is too heavy a price
for being wrong. If anything, resisters are trying to keep the
Establishment from fulfilling *its* prophecy.

I'll forgive you a little arrogance. But Wallace didn't run as
strong as expected and a new administration is in. That could
mean a fresh start of sorts. As somebody put it, "the whole
world pauses over an American election."
It won't pause for long. It's too early to be factual about
Richard Nixon. Let's try rather to understand that no man

of the people can be elected President these days. Some political weathervanes claim that the last feeble hope of reform died with Robert Kennedy and with Eugene Mc-Carthy's rejection. Others believe—I among them—that if either had prevailed to the Presidency, he would have simply delayed the reckoning. They were the best the political process could produce and hope to win with—yet neither of them took special risks for the truth: one met a bullet, another met Richard Daley and Lyndon Johnson. They are casualties of political immobility and political intransigence. To be more precise, political leadership is immensely sure-footed and responsive while representing economic power. While representing the real needs of people, it is bankrupt. Those who run the country see to it that politicians are sure things. Kennedy and McCarthy were not sure things.

You're saying that Mr. Nixon is a sure thing?
Surer than another Johnson Administration. Humphrey is as imperialist as most, but he helped Lyndon Johnson to botch the Viet Nam job, to put in jeopardy our "national unity," that precious euphemism. In other words, he helped to put a long-haul strain on the dollar for short-term profits. (The dollar is, you know, the basic adhesive of our society; it is the greatest source of "national unity.")

Let me understand you. Are you saying that power gets the kind of political leadership it demands? And that this is political unrepresentation?
That's nearly it. And the common vote means something only if people are tapped into the patronage system. Most people are, which makes it so enormously and dangerously effective. I say "dangerously" because, humanly speaking, it's death-dealing, even to those sharing its rewards.
You might remember Cordell Hull saying during World War II that "the political lineup follows the economic lineup." Now, in that reference, he explained why various nations

joined either the Allied or Axis camps. But it applies to
internal politics as well; corporate power manages to get
politicians that will best represent its interests. No more
public checks and balances, and a great deal more exploitation and terror. That's why dissenters get hyperbolic about
it. The single-mindedness of American plutocrats about pro-
duction-consumption, investments, mergers, expansion and
power has deprived them of alternatives. Greed has been
institutionalized, presenting us with a problem of unrepresentative—and therefore illegitimate—power.

Let me say this as well, at the risk of becoming tiresome.
Since we are an economic, political and military empire,
there is a nexus between foreign and domestic unrest. Foreign policy is two things—profits and pacification. So it is at
home. Disagree with business (or its supporting operations
like the military), stick up your protesting head in a threatening way, and you'll be pacified. Just like our blacks. So it
seems that uprisings, in the U.S. and abroad, will be similar,
stemming from those who would dispose of profits differently
(like for themselves), and those who dislike pacification.
They're usually the same people.

Hence the observation by people that revolution will be
"back-to-back," violent, sustained and very painful. Overseas
opposition at present is strong and growing stronger—in
Southeast Asia and, in ominous fashion, Latin America.
Whereas opposition at home lies largely dormant, government treats it very delicately. It can't be bludgeoned with
the same ruthlessness that it is abroad.

*I'm trying to find a label for your analysis. It offends me.
You know, same domestic and foreign policy, same exploitation with a military or a police backup, same human reaction
everywhere, same rising violence everywhere. There's an*
absolution *about it, . . . that's not the word. . . .*
Maybe *generic* is. A human rights background does that for

one, I guess. It seems to me that people react to injustice in substantially similar ways, when they know about it. And today, they're learning about what they have and what they need at a phenomenal rate. The technological capitalism which empowers this country to mobilize its enormous capital and military resources also educates the masses. The interests of empire and the interests of "feeder" states conflict; control and nationalism conflict. And because neither can help itself (neocapitalisms must expand or die, and people will seek alternatives to misery), the two will collide. In this sense, profits inspire revolution and become death warrants. They generate too much violence to be viable.

I suppose you would claim that American policy expresses a philosophy of power, while you express a philosophy of man? That's putting it bluntly indeed. To say that altruism is lacking in official policy, even in Vietnam, is simply untrue. I'm trying to say that policy takes its dominant direction from an élitist conception of national interest, which is, essentially, national income and prosperity.

Furthermore, it is not my philosophy of man that is in question. It is rather that of our men of power. Personally, some are warm, intelligent and humane men, who read Camus, Schweitzer and John XXIII with understanding and sympathy. As John Kennedy and Robert McNamara did. But what would have been Kennedy's desserts if he had not risked nuclear war over Cuba? Impeachment, likely. So power bureaucracies are often like tails wagging dogs. And loyalty to them is insured by the fact that bureaucracies *work* for bureaucrats. They do not work for people equally, but they work for the managers and technicians who run them. If by some magical stroke one could force bureaucracies to fit the needs of children first, they might be more impartial.

You're obviously anti-bureaucratic. That means you're anti-technological as well, since the achievements of technology

can't be applied without bureaucracies (and bureaucrats).
I have nothing against bureaucracies as such, or technology
as such. I merely question the spirit that now occupies them;
a spirit quite counter to their rhetoric. Hence the credibility
gap. I have known bureaucracies that were human enough.
Admittedly, they were not very large ones. And I know that
technology has impressive human achievements, though its
overwhelming contribution has been in the service of war.
This is too good to let pass. A student wrote the following
about the bureaucratic spirit, and the technological spirit
which it controls. He calls summit bureaucrats "Bigees."
"The Bigees are a small group of men. Little about them is
known. They are probably old. They possess wealth surpass-
ing the bounds of imagination. They have no real needs or
desires, but cultivate avarice as a sort of obsessive hobby.
They sit in smoke-filled rooms, so it may be presumed that
they smoke cigars. In the councils of the Bigees, one might
hear decisions that one thought no one could make. Buy
Uruguay. Sell Bolivia. Hold India. Pollute New York. The
decisions are of incomprehensible variety, but they have in
common the fact that they are swiftly implemented and invariably soak the Little Man." "Why We're Against the
Bigees" James S. Kunen, *Atlantic, October,* 1968.)

*I'll get back to the student rebellion later, if you don't mind.
But first I'd like to ask you about their place in the revolution, or the Second Civil War, or whatever you choose to
call it. Marcuse says there won't be any revolution here,
because a student-worker coalition is impossible. The workers don't need a revolution.*
Marcuse is a Marxist, and he understands well the Marxist
blueprint for violent revolution. But sometimes I think he
gets dogmatic about comparisons. He says the students
failed in France because the workers copped out on them.
He's certainly right. But France isn't the United States. We

have in common with France an advanced industrial society, but many differences distinguish us. And the difference might make the difference, so to speak.

Who's going to replace the workers then? There has to be a foreseeable revolutionary force, whatever its elements. Who's going to make it up?
No one knows precisely. But I do know that, paradoxically, the Vietnamese have educated us as to what Americanism is—its materialism, mythology, violence and ambition. Students have been most receptive; the antiwar movement began on the campuses, largely. Now the education has spread to the black liberation movement, which learned not only from the Vietnamese, but from Malcolm X, from Dr. King's murder, and from police repression. People like the Black Panthers now understand that they have much more in common with the oppressed overseas than with white Americans. Excepting of course, white radicals, with whom they have identified a common adversary—bankers, industrial barons, and their political mouthpieces.

Students and blacks then. Who else?
Draft resisters, certainly, and they are not all students. Of course, it remains to be seen if they will repeat their first revolutionary "no" after release. Intellectuals also, who are learning that truth unchallenged by life—their lives or student's lives—is not living. Then there's the Church, which is relearning its Gospel in the agony of renewal by decree, even the decrees of Vatican II. Note the Vietnamese people, which says something about that the American Catholic bishops are finally "questioning" the Viet Nam war.

Almost nobody refers to the Church as a revolutionary force, least of all churchmen. Most true humanists look upon the Church as a boil upon the buttocks of progress, if you'll pardon the expression.
No offense—it's too painfully true. For a long time now my

brother and I have been at vantage points observing our official brand of philanthropy—its affluence, racism and service of the state. But there are signs this is changing—no credit to us, but to our blacks and the Vietnamese people.

Let's return to the students for a moment. How well do you know students, and how critical are movements like SDS?
I don't know them as well as I should, though most of my speaking has been done on campuses. That's my loss, not theirs. It's impossible to overstress their importance—they are the national hope. I sometimes feel this so deeply that I wonder why more aren't in the Movement; or why, especially in the Midwest, they join the Young Americans for Freedom, a vapid, right-of-center outfit; or why they cop out by running to Canada. And this is immensely unfair. If the middle generation stands for anything in value or views, it's largely because of the students. I would not be in jail without them. They shamed me, I cannot say how much.

How accurate is, say, the SDS appraisal of this society? They certainly lack both organization and program.
It's very accurate, given their resources. They have very little Christian vitality to draw on, you know. So they write their own gospel—it's a secular one, but very moral. Added to this, the best of them have an insatiable hunger for spirituality, and they will devour it when they find it. As my brother says, "They eat real priests whole." And typically, they seek out a man like Chardin, often on their own. And eat the book so to speak.
As for their appraisal of this society, what could be as moral, poignant and real as these student words again from Mr. Kunen's article: "This isn't a free country. You can't drop out of school because you'd be drafted, and you have to study certain things to get a degree, and you have to get a degree to make it, and you have to make it to get what you want, and you can't even decide what you want, because it's

all programmed into you beforehand. You can say whatever you want, but you won't be heard because the media control that, but if you do manage to be heard, the People won't like it, because the people have been told what to like. And if they don't like you, they might even kill you, because the government endorses killing by exemplification."

Magnificent? And pitiable that a great young person would have to say this about his society, the society we have handed him. Yet if students have someone halfway human to work with, they will walk to hell and back with him. Sometimes even alone, like David Miller, Suzi Williams, Bruce Dancis and Frank Femia—all in jail now. I remember one student who hitchhiked from Minnesota to visit us in jail for 15 minutes, and to say "thank you" with tears streaming down his cheeks. And another who quietly rejected his student deferment as he entered senior year in a stuffy Catholic college. He went quietly to jail, with no one to advise him, support him, stand by him.

Yet the charge still exists SDS doesn't have an organization to speak of, and the program they offer to replace institutions is either nonexistent or childish. Nor do they shrink from violence. Doesn't this argue to a lot of immaturity and inexperience?

Not really. As a study in contrast, the high priests of government, business and church have us walking a nuclear tightrope with no net; have us collaborating with Third World rape; have us acquiescing in genocide in Vietnam, and then ask the students, "Where's your organization, where's your program, where's your nonviolence?" They asked Dr. King that, and when he offered them organization, program and nonviolence they killed him anyway. Vicariously, of course. Many "straights" from the over-30 generations have excoriated young people as filthy, pot-high, lascivious and shiftless —sort of white nigger types, because they have not taken our guilt from us and haven't done it painlessly; haven't given us a clean, orderly revolution with none of a revolution's pain.

Why don't young radicals have an organization; why do people look for "the leadership" at SDS headquarters in Chicago (and find nobody in, more likely than not)?
Because they trying to beat the American "leader" myth, the "hero" cult which implies that only a few divinely endowed types, chosen by due suffrage, are qualified to lead and rule and save the great unwashed. They rather say that this kind of upgraded Daniel Booneism has taken us to the brink. Let's all be responsible, they say. Which is a fairly firm approach.
As for a program, what revolution worthy of the name has ever had a program? Except to right the wrongs of the old, tired, decadent order? Our Declaration of Independence grew out of the struggle for human rights and political independence; the Cuban and North and South Vietnamese social programs grew out of the liberation struggle. Tyranny taught the revolutionaries what people need is justice. Asking young radicals for a program is like asking a patient what kind of health he wants, or a black person what kind of freedom he wants. The Establishment doesn't want another program—it has its own. It wants control.

One last question. People look upon you, your brother, Tom Lewis and the Melvilles as desperate types who have lost hope. Is there any hope? Or has war gained tenure for itself, simply because balances of power demand it, wordly economy demands it, and no surrogate has been found for it?
There is great hope because the moral question of world community is also the political question of survival; the moral question of conscience is also the political question of self-determination. Historically, this is an entirely new phenomenon, and they constitute basic lessons for both East

and West. The Soviets must democratize, and they must allow the satellite empire to go its own way. The U.S. must socialize, or face internal disruption and chaos. These lessons are breaking down the curtains, people are learning them very rapidly. Time, however, is of the essence. As long as tension exists over crimes like Viet Nam and Czechoslovakia, the nuclear sword remains poised.

Thank you for taking the time. Next time, I'll ask the questions and you can answer. But I warn you—My question will be better than yours.

Thank you! That's a deal. And my answers will be better than yours.

November 20

IN PRAISE OF TOM LEWIS

The other prisoners say that Tom Lewis is my "rap partner," or that I am his—meaning that we are partners in crime. Apart from "crime," we have experienced much together— pain, joy, fear, celebration. Perhaps because of this, people find us puzzling—they find it hard to understand a relationship that is so casual, matter-of-fact, and free. Unfortunately, there is little chance to explain that we have had our "brush" with the powers of this world, an encounter that has helped us to remain unscathed and to become unchained. The powers have conceded us a piece of "liberated turf," our own persons in jail.

Tom sits in the next cell in Baltimore County Jail, reading, writing, talking with our cellmates, or working patiently on a new painting. There are no problems for me with Tom —I suspect he has more with me—no regrets, despondency, or cynicism. With him, one never gets that appalling feeling of being over one's head because he is over his; of suggesting an eventuality for which he was unequipped; of introducing him to a turning point too mercilessly, when emotion and mind and heart were unequal to the test. If anything, Tom Lewis welcomes crisis, there's no need to hold his hand in the dark.

I remember when he first came to visit me in Baltimore, to which I had recently been transferred, a casualty of official sanctions, removed abruptly from seminary teaching because of my dissent on the war. Since it was clear that Tom was searching for something real, however, I was prompted to offer something better than wound-licking. He was considering the priesthood, but it seemed that studies would be too long and freedom too short for him to persevere in such a course. A seminary did not seem the place for a man already grappling with the raw stuff of human survival—poverty, race, and war. More likely, it would be a distraction and a waste.

I learned important things about Tom—about his art, his street work with CORE, his fidelity to the Church, his dislike of the Viet Nam war, a dislike that would later turn to horror. Very shortly, we worked together in weekly demonstrations with CORE, and he went to jail in connection with a housing sit-in. Without knowing it, we were learning to read and write, learning a gospel that was rarely preached in the subtle, ruthless, churchgoing centers of our society. That is to say, we were learning about power, and also about a power with which to confront it.

We read history, economics, political science, sociology, and above all, the documents of Vatican II. I began to organize the parish slums, to lecture again, and to write a book. And Tom emerged to leadership in CORE, became deeply involved with peace organizations, and began to receive serious recognition as a vital contemporary artist. (He has been exhibiting professionally at juried shows since he was nineteen.)

Our critical reading and growing experience provided terrible lessons, nightmares that destroyed the placid surfaces of a naïve consciousness. We began to realize that we hadn't known our country, that we had been duped by its mythology, that we had been infants at the feet of power, that we had actually worked to sustain its deceptions.

But we learned. We learned to accept a deaf-and-dumb Church and still love it; to be spit upon in the streets and take abuse from every quarter; to probe consciences gently and ungently; to lose old friends, and to make new ones; to appreciate fear, including our own; and to prepare for the real thing—disgrace, jail, even worse.

But "we" is not to the point here, while Tom is. He is a difficult man to capture in print, partly because he is reluctant to talk about himself. He acts as if his extraordinary commitment to others was commonplace, as if his life style was typical. He is not easy to describe because he has accepted the Gospel not as an impossible ideal but as an experience too precious for anybody to miss. And partly because he is an artist, with an artist's trust in his work.

In the spring of 1964 Tom went to a Baltimore whites-only amusement park that CORE had decided to desegregate. He began, not as a participant but as an artist: "I went, sketchbook in hand, but while standing in the angry crowd of white bigots, sketching the demonstrators, I suddenly realized that my passivism in that particular situation *actually made me a part of that mob.* The crowd was shouting, jeering, and cursing at the demonstrators, while the police were dragging some of them away. I went up to a black marshal in charge of the picket line, and when he asked why I wanted to join, I told him very honestly that I was ashamed to be white. He smiled at the answer and gave me a sign."

Gwyn Oak Amusement Park was a road to Damascus for Tom Lewis—he had few doubts about his future after that, allowing events and experience to carry him along. As his grasp of American irresponsibility became firmer, so did his dissent—until he found himself a federal prisoner with a six-year sentence, and with unresolved and serious charges from the state of Maryland as well. A simple story when presented this way, but the interim contained enormous resolution, and difficulties compounded by the sensibilities and perceptions of an artist.

I asked him how he handled his fear, since I knew that he had plenty to fear. "It seems to me that faith stands behind conviction, and that conviction stands behind courage. One acts because one believes. What do I believe? Above all, that Christ's Incarnation happened, and because it happened, it never ends. He is being reborn in man always, but only through men. So I am an instrument. Plenty of things have nourished my faith—a devout family, the liturgical renewal, my own Christian art. But two things above all—the Gospel and what Christians call community. They finally led me out of religious liberalism into Christian radicalism."

His personal life came under the same exhaustive logic. With a huge talent for enjoying people, he lived a wholesome and fulfilling social life. *But* always within the Movement—there could be no vacations from it, even for an occasional date. Naturally, this awoke my curiosity, and we discussed it often enough to piece together the following: "A middle-class marriage means adopting the surrounding life style, however sterile that might be. I can't accept such a standard, simply because it is irrelevant to what is happening. Marriage is not a primary vocation; being a Christian is. Ideally, a marriage should help a couple grow in revolutionary witness against man's abuse of man. Otherwise, how can one reconcile it with Christianity? It would take a revolutionary type to interest me enough to consider marriage. I no longer have the time or the money to court a conventionally decent girl—the idea holds no attraction for me. This may seem utopian, but I am convinced that, eventually, the Movement will supply me with a wife. Even if it doesn't, that will be for the best."

It has been well said that if one is for justice, one also has to be for revolution. The classical injustices today come from built-in disparities of wealth and poverty, power and impotence. To confront these phenomena in the national scene, Tom feels, "An ordinary type of armed struggle is useless, because power is programmed to crush any move toward violent revolution. Nevertheless, conventional politics cannot bring justice: Even the honest are politicians too firmly wedded to the captains of finance and industry. There is nothing left but creative nonviolence, directed toward the great abuses of American power—the draft, military hardware and personnel, financial centers, and defense industry. If people resisting overseas make investments less profitable, and if people here make business too expensive to run normally, you'll see more concessions than you'll know what to do with. And out of them, justice will be won."

"You know," he said whimsically, "power can't handle nonviolence. The Pentagon is studying it and trying to co-opt it, but that's useless. Power is clever, but its cleverness is stereotyped and sterile and computerized. Power can't deal with grace and creativity. If it tries, it will have to send its computers into therapy."

"Yes," he reflected, "the revolution in this country will have no parallel in history. There are few textbooks and fewer lessons for what we have to do. Nonetheless, this revolution might well be as useful to the world as 1776 was."

"Of course, for me the Movement lies at the heart of everything. Not that it's perfect; at present it sometimes lacks honesty, could do with a lot less rhetoric, and is often hung up with its own image. But without the Movement there would be nothing. Catholics are finally getting into it, and that's hopeful. Maybe they are the only group with enough sense of suffering and enough cohesion to make a difference. After all, they made the difference in France during the Algerian crisis."

I have learned at some expense, as have others, that when Tom Lewis speaks seriously, it is well to listen. He knows the psychology of structured violence, has good political sense, enjoys the play of ideas, and is a fine tactician. There are nearly twenty years separating us, but I have learned to listen. He is a cautious revolutionary—that is to say, he combines remarkably the virtues of wisdom and prophecy. How many times has he curbed my impetuosity, advising me quietly to look for better evidence?

One of our friends said some time ago, "One cleric in the news is worth ten students, or ten of us." Unfortunately, there's much truth in this, but it remains a greater indictment of the clergy than of those docile laymen who have been trained to wait for a lead from Father So-and-so rather than step out on their own. Clerics have been so protected from everyday reality, and so ready to bless the powers of government and finance with silence and immobility, that any departure from such a sickening pattern is indeed news. In contrast, those laymen who are trying to find their way as Christians must usually go alone and unrepresented, relying upon grace, experience, and events to teach them the appropriate response. An independent like Tom Lewis will leave the headlines to the clerics, thankful that *someone* will protest with him.

When one looks for the qualities that make a man truly contemporary, simplicity and disciplined complexity are near the top of the list. Lewis is that rare person who exemplifies both. I recall one scene that may serve to illustrate his worth. One Sunday afternoon after our first conviction, four of us—two priests and two laymen—had plunged into a familiar routine, analyzing the Great Society and worrying about possible alternatives. As usual, the clerics dominated the conversation—on this occasion, with more facility than sense; Tom listened with growing exasperation and finally exploded. "All this talk is meaningless," he insisted, "unless you act on what you say, feel, and believe. History has taught us about the apathy of the Church in Nazi Germany. We've agreed that the war in Viet Nam is genocidal. Unless we act, we might as well say that Catholicism in the United States is meaningless. As for myself, I am moving against this war, even if it means doing it alone."

A few weeks later, before receiving a sentence of six years for pouring blood on draft files at the Customs House, he spoke more formally: "I stand here in moral outrage, as a witness against what is being done by my government to the poor. The poor not only in America, but in Viet Nam, Thailand, Laos, Guatemala, Bolivia—to the poor in more than eighty foreign countries. . . .

"As a man, as a Christian, as an artist, I believe that Jesus Christ has flowered in man's humanity. To be human is to love; to claim humanity is to treat all men as brothers. This is fundamental, whether these brothers are white, black, or yellow—South Americans, Israelis, Chinese, or Vietnamese.

"If I am guilty of loving men as brothers . . .

"If I am guilty of believing that democracy is a system by which its people have a meaningful voice . . .

"If I am guilty of taking the New Testament and the Catholic Church seriously—then I welcome a sentence."

The prosecution of Tom Lewis rests.

November 24

THE LAST SUNDAY AFTER PENTECOST

Without looking for it, we here in Baltimore County Jail have a mutual-admiration society going with two priests and several seminarians from St. Mary's, Roland Park, the nearby Sulpician seminary. The warden brings them in to offer the Eucharist every Sunday, which they do with imagination and warmth. For our part, we try to play the role of bloody-but-unbowed, thereby fulfilling some indefinable yet basic need in our clerical friends. One young theological student, his Irish face suffused with feeling, devotedly told me, "You guys are where all of us belong." Whereupon Tom Lewis gives me the elbow and speculates, "We might get us a radical from this bunch yet."

The celebrant today, Father Jim Finley from Brooklyn, asked me to share a dialogue homily with himself and several others. The Gospel was from the twenty-fourth chapter of Matthew, and its theme was hope. Everyone had something to say about hope, with Advent beginning the following Sunday. And everyone tried to understand what we knew to be true—that Jesus Christ is the hope of mankind, of these times, and of this nation.

I said something about Bishop Pike, and how it took his son's suicide to help him regain his faith and hope, or substantial portions of them. I would be unfair to Pike if I said that he had lost belief in the hereafter. Rather, he took the position that Christians cannot be sure—that there is no empirical evidence for life after death. At any rate, after his suicide in New York City, young Pike supplied evidence by manipulating certain signs of his presence in the Pike apartment in England, signs discovered and recognized by his father upon return there. The bishop responded by contacting a medium, who arranged communication with his son.

Few will find fault with Pike's hope in man—he has stood for a questioning and socially relevant Christianity for years. Now his present hope in God, and in a future with God, has been strengthened by a son who is dead, but who, against all expectations, has become an instrument of hope for his father. In a word, the young man accomplished what the commonly accepted authority of scripture could not: "I am the resurrection, and the life; he that believeth in me, though he were dead, yet shall he live; and whosoever liveth and believeth in me shall never die. Believest thou this?" (John 11:25–27.)

In contrast to Pike's quality of hope, there are the examples of others like Gandhi and Hammarskjöld. Neither was a formal believer, as Pike is, but both were prepared to go beyond him in sacrifice for man. For Gandhi, the rationale was a simple one of self-realization, the hope of seeing God "face to face." And Hammarskjöld, revered as a martyr by his colleagues in the UN, wrote in 1960, ten months before his death in the Congo: "For him who looks towards the future, the Manger is situated on Golgotha, and the Cross has already been raised in Bethlehem. Strive, the pains of death endure, peace eternal to secure."

Pike tried to harmonize rationalism with his hope, while most Christians tend to superstition in theirs. One is a humanist failing; the other deistic. Both tend to be unfaithful to Christ, who spoke of the last things only in a context dominated by the Judgment: "For I was hungry and you gave me to eat." Our Lord, it would seem, wished to emphasize that hope must correspond both to divine sonship and to human brotherhood. To center one's hope in man is to compromise the main expressions of hope—optimism, sacrifice, and death. And to center one's hope in God is to risk egotism, withdrawal, and despair.

Paradoxically, as throughout the world purely human reasons for hope decrease, Christian reasons increase. Therefore, Christians ought to be outstanding for their hope. For those of us who are American, this constitutes a painfully priceless lesson. For America's hope is in its power, power whose definition is the imperial nation-state, whose spirit is capitalist aggrandizement, and whose force is technology.

And power whose enormity is, in fact, equalled only by its impotence.

Such power tends to destroy, since it cannot remain powerful unless it subdues the will of others to resist. In our world this has become less and less possible, as Viet Nam strikingly shows—just as the failure to subdue resistance fosters the tendency to crush resisters. Which invites the threat of having no one left to exploit. Hence, stalemate and a Paris negotiating table.

Pope Paul says that the new name of peace is development. This is true, but everything depends on one's understanding of development. Of this I am at least sure: Hope is nonviolent resistance, rebellion, and revolution. It has always been so, though never has the lesson been so forcefully taught. And this is hopeful.

November 25

Another situation-report to clarify our plight or good fortune, whatever people might decide to call it. We have been in Baltimore County Jail since September 4—no outside exercise, no chance to enjoy the fine fall weather. Jail facilities do not allow these extravagances, and we do not crave privileges that other inmates cannot enjoy. These are facts of existence that do not depress us—we chose them when we chose civil disobedience.

This cellblock is home, at least for the present. Three times a day we leave it for meals that are barely sufficient, yet are relished with appetite and humor. We keep strong by daily calisthenics and keep spiritually alive by prayer, reading, and writing. Hopefully, we have grown neither stale nor soft in this interim.

We wait for a bail hearing, set sometime for the week of

December 8. Denied bail four times already (usually granted automatically on a conviction under appeal), prospects appear slightly better now. And we have decided to accept bail if we are given the opportunity.

As one gets deeper into nonviolent dissent, decisions tend to become more intricate and more difficult. Acceptance or rejection of bail? Case in point. Who has ever rejected bail? There is no precedent, and when one talks about setting one, most people are tempted to tap their foreheads. Public and legal opinion, plus the outrage of defendants, limits exceptions to virtual nonexistence.

We have no interest in setting a precedent, since we are impelled by a deeper rationality. How does one identify with those enslaved by tyranny or greed? How does one truly aid the powerless, except by choosing powerlessness? And the most urgent question: How does one free the Holy Spirit for His work of reconciliation and peace? In jail, or out? If we stayed in, we could at least illustrate the injustice of our punishment; we could illustrate our right to bail by first securing it and then refusing it.

At the point of final decision, however, our friends intervened. They wanted us out. They wanted us out because they suffer over separation more than we do, a gift embarrassing to us but that reflects their profound generosity. We have to listen to them, owing them what we do. Some of them had influenced us to civil disobedience; others had supported us by choosing it themselves. Therefore, if the government offers bail, a community will accept it.

Meanwhile, the state of Maryland resolutely pursues its plans for us. Sometime in the New Year, it will charge us with conspiracy, sabotage, destruction of property, assault upon persons, etc. The charges expand or contract from time to time, depending on imponderables like public opinion, letters to the editor, and firm or slack bowels in the DA's office. As it stands now, all preliminary motions must be filed by January 2. Following them, we will probably go to trial before the end of March.

The contempt we feel for such vicious nonsense defies explanation—but we try to keep it under control. The officials most responsible for our indictment are dangerous "little men," but they have the grandeur of the law behind them, and solid public opinion. We have no choice but to take them seriously.

Double jeopardy? Certainly, a second trial for the same "crimes." Will we be convicted? Probably; people often receive a second conviction in similar circumstances. In cases of "immediate danger"—which the government arbitrarily defines—federal law enforcement will team up with the state, or the state with the city, to convict with double penalties. Quite frequently a man will serve one prison sentence, to be jailed again for the same crime upon release.

One of our lawyers is anxious to go to court, convinced that we can win. Winning or losing, however, is not important to us, any more than it was in federal court. More important are the reasons why the law becomes a deterrent weapon in the hands of power—like a fist in a velvet glove. We suspect that we know why, and we intend to talk about our suspicions at the trial.

November 26

A new friend arrives to stay with us until the federal marshals take him to a federal penitentiary. He is twenty-two, a draft resister—all hair, eyes, and spirit. He talks to us like an old and trusted friend, conveying the peace and simplicity of a child.

A drop-out from a Midwestern state university, he has followed the road for two years, a pilgrim and, I'm sure, an apostle. "I'm not for organizations much—they seem to run people more than people run them. 'My thing' is talking to people, but I usually end up listening. Maybe that's more important. Yet what surprises me is the fact that I often get people very mad. I guess my looks make them afraid, and when I talk, they get more and more uptight.

"A Klansman wanted to kill me in Florida. I was hitch-hiking north from Gainesville, and he picked me up. We got to talking, and like Southerners do, he got onto black people. I said a few things and they made him mad. He started to rave about killing 'niggers,' said he'd kill me too if he thought he could get away with it. Told me to look in the back seat, and sure enough, there was a heavy rifle and a shotgun.

"Then a woman passed him fast and cut in to miss a truck coming. He got madder yet and started to tailgate her, actually hitting her car in the rear several times. At eighty miles an hour—that poor woman! Then he stopped for gas and kicked me out. Later, I was hitchhiking down the road, and he just roared by, giving me the finger."

Our friend refused induction by failing to show up. Then, with no lawyer, he defended himself on grounds of the Thirteenth Amendment—involuntary servitude. When they found him guilty and jailed him, he began to fast, refusing both food and water. "It wasn't just my sentence [4½ years]; it was that city jail they took me to. It was bedlam, dig? I'm against jails, see, but there are jails and there are jails. This one was a gasser. Anyway, after four days, I couldn't get up without going into a spin and falling. My mouth got so dry, I was afraid to swallow, afraid of strangling. They got shook and asked me where I wanted to go. I said here, so they took me out on a stretcher."

The evening he arrived, he celebrated his victory with a little water and went to bed. He looked supremely contented, sleeping soundly despite all the lights and noise. In the morning he ate with concentrated purpose and joy. But after two days of us and TV, he asked for isolation. As he left he told me, "I love people, but essentially I'm a loner. I have to have silence for meditation every now and then. See you guys."

One of our veteran cons, who had seen more of state prison "holes" than any man I know, paid him this tribute: "He's a born protester!"

November 28

It is Thanksgiving evening as I begin this, and we have just come from downstairs and a bountiful turkey dinner. The facts at hand ought to make us grateful—good health, full stomachs, clean quarters, comfortable beds for the night. Instead, an unhealthy mixture of gloom and tension prevails, smoldering like a fire of damp refuse and breaking out fitfully. One inmate broods over an angry letter to his family; another curses a waiter and goes sullenly off to the "hole"; another glares balefully at his food and baits a youngster across the table.

Just something to ride out, I guess—jailhouse neurosis. Separation from one's family does this; so do problems caused and left behind; so do shame, bitterness, and alienation—on both sides of these bars.

But not entirely. The unrest of my friends at Thanksgiving —or Christmas or Easter—goes wider and deeper than estrangement from their families, guilt, and frustration. I believe that it also bears some relation to the Great Society and its awesome ability to infiltrate and control almost everywhere—even in this cellblock. It never relaxes its hold on these men; locks and bars do not shut out its cultural flotsam. Quid bono? Madison Avenue has well-tilled ground here, as do cold-war propaganda and white-supremacist fantasies.

It suddenly strikes me, with the force and misery of a

coronary, that our friends are eager to rejoin and participate in the Great Society—even in a "socially deviant" way. Hope for a family reunion—the redressing of past mistakes—contributes only superficially to their eagerness. What they miss —as a junkie misses his fix—is their larger family engrossed in the intoxicating business of "making it": easy money, new marvels from Detroit, new mysteries in cans, new and more casual sex—the whole, massive, hustling operation of a society cemented together by mendacity and aggrandizement.

"What about victims?" one might ask. "What about employers, friends, or enemies?" What about them, indeed. "They'll take it from somebody else." As though to say: "You miss the point, Jack. Bread and circuses in the Great Society means you take them. They're there, but you gotta take them. See?"

I put a check rein on my speculations. What's bugging me? Is it overempathy, self-pity, or just plain snobbery? Or is it a kind of cynicism which sees demons in every human enterprise? Perplexed and dejected, I pick up the evening paper and run into the following pieces of Americana, a litany of thanks from a spokesman for the Great Society. During the next year, he says:

1. More than 195,675,000 Americans will not be arrested;
2. More than 115,262,000 individuals will maintain a formal affiliation with some religious group;
3. More than 8,161,000 of our young men will not burn their draft cards;
4. More than 3,050,000 of our young men will honorably serve in the military;
5. More than 199,835,000 of our people will not be identified with subversive causes;
6. More than 48,315,000 students will not riot or petition to destroy our system;
7. More than 2,225,000 teachers and professors will not strike or participate in demonstrations;

8. More than 75,000,000 citizens and corporations will pay more than $148 billion in wages and salaries. Their total income will exceed $620 billion;

10. More than $42 billion will be added to all kinds of personal savings;

11. More of our people will earn more, spend more, save more, and live better than ever before.*

The article, written by a Hearst functionary, is a crude, widely endorsed package of the assumptions that make our neocapitalist paradise tick, namely:

1. that the unarrested are guiltless and law-abiding;

2. that church affiliation contributes morally to personal and public life;

3. that young men should not burn their draft cards, though war threatens humanity;

4. that young men who refuse military service are dishonorable;

5. that "causes" aiming at fundamental change are necessarily bad for the nation;

6. that students who riot or petition intend to destroy our system; or if they do, that this is necessarily bad for the nation;

7. that teachers and professors should never strike or participate in demonstrations;

8. that federal taxes should be paid unquestioningly;

9 and 10. that $620 billion in personal income, and $42 billion in savings, is an unmixed good in a starving world.

11. that earning more, spending more, saving more, and living better are "progress," even if they cost us filthy air and water, carnage on the highways, ghetto decay and suburban mediocrity, foreign war and domestic unrest, better

* Charles L. Gould, publisher, *San Francisco Examiner; Baltimore News American,* Nov. 28, 1968, p. 8-A.

bombs and rising war budgets—all for life in a technological wasteland.

What's the connection between my friends here in jail and a plutocratic mouthpiece for the Great Society? His values, his message, his readers—and his masters in the board rooms—have helped to put my friends here, will help to keep them here, and will, when ready, return them to the streets to pick up their lives where they dropped them at arrest. That is to say, they will return these men to jail, not once or twice, but in the case of most, repeatedly.

As institutions (like Great Society art and Great Society wars), federal and local penal systems are organically consistent with the Great Society itself. This is the tragedy of prisoners, and also of prison officials, who believe profoundly in rehabilitation—education, recreation, Christian inquiry, job training, work release, weekends for the married, and so on. The warden here is one of these dedicated people.

But a fundamental question needs to be raised: "What does rehabilitation mean?" Does it mean readying a man for protest against the insanity outside, or does it mean asking him to be merely a cog? It is not by chance that we encounter such friendliness and understanding from fellow inmates, mostly black. They speak of exorbitant sentences and delayed trials, of no counsel and no money. Whatever they have done, whether the charge is addiction, burglary, or assault, it is ultimately part of the immemorial protest of blacks against a society which seems unable to accept them as people. It used to be that protest was fasting, malingering, or the terrible vengeance of Nat Turner. Today it is crime, James Johnson (one of the Fort Hood Three), Carmichael, Newark and Detroit.

So we protest together; if only we had more time to tell the brothers of this. Because a country which cannot welcome its black people, cannot leave the Vietnamese alone, cannot temper overseas economic greed, cannot but slide from the Bomb to the ABM systems, and then preach solemnly about law and order.

People must have the power to be people, or they will seize it. Either case can well be called revolution.

A PRIEST
IN THE RESISTANCE:
AN INTERVIEW

This section of interview with Philip Berrigan was placed at the end of THE PRISON JOURNALS because of its more ideological and personal nature. The other parts of the book structure a man in relation to his experience in a physical setting and are a proper preparation to the personal thoughts found here.

Q. *Could you describe what your sacramental life as a priest has been in the past, and how it might have been changed by your experience in jail?*

A. Well, I think that my sacramental life has always been largely conventional. Even in Newburgh in 1965, when I was already seriously into the peace issue, I used to say mass daily, and I would go to confession pretty much on a weekly basis. And this continued on into my Baltimore days, because I was in a parish where people needed the Eucharist every day. And then, too, because it was quite an advanced parish, both liturgically and socially. On Sundays a lot of whites would come, not only from the city itself, but even from out of state. They would be progressive Catholics looking for good liturgy and a good homily, or they'd be peace people looking for a more serious orientation for their own lives, and wanting to discuss issues. Today I go to confession maybe once every three months. Of course, there's an entirely new approach to confession now, and this has affected all Catholics. The orientation in my confession is largely how I might have failed in my responsibilities toward people, especially those who are involved in communities of witness, who are on the borderline of risk, and who are in the process of commending themselves to the Gospel in a very serious way—which, according to the present jargon, means an entirely new life style. How I have failed in my responsibilities there, and of course one's failures are always manifold, because it's an entirely new dimension, it's very, very difficult, it's very abrasive. You're dealing with such a wide spectrum of ideology—political analysis, conscience, emotiveness, all these things. The ideal preparation would be to sit with a friend and talk it out. But the only person I've found that I could do this with would be my brother Dan. Failing the opportunity to do that with him on a frequent basis—though I suppose I could get the opportunity if I really attempted to organize it—I go to a Jesuit confessor in the center of Baltimore. And I go through a rather conventional thing.

Q. *What does the sacrament of penance mean to you, as an experience or as a need?*

A. Well, of course, I still believe profoundly in the dimension of grace, which is imparted through the sacrament. And all of the allied things on which grace depends—atonement, retribution, sacrifice, and the development of new attitudes toward the future, the making of a new present in order to secure a better future. I still believe very powerfully in these. And they suggest what I'm looking for.

And the Eucharist is still quite central to my life. I usually either offer the Eucharist with friends, or else I offer a very truncated and very reflective Eucharist in my room, at my desk, almost daily. And that means a long scriptural meditation, and a very, very short public-oriented offertory, and then the consecration.

Q. *How would you describe your discipline of prayer?*
A. I conceive of prayer as a reflection upon the divine operation in the human community, and the relationship of God to man, and out of that, of man to man. Reflections upon this, and dealing with whatever insights have come from the New Testament, mostly; and renewed dedication in terms of responsibility to the needs of the human community, which I conceive of increasingly in universal terms.

Q. *How has your stay in prison affected your sacramental life?*
A. I think it might have clarified it a great deal in the sense that one is thrust into a new role in prison, one is forced to grope for a new justification for one's presence in prison. You have to rationalize it because you have to extract hope from it, and this is a very living need. It isn't so much a straight-ahead, ongoing process as it is a matter of being humbled, starting all over, looking for maybe the right questions. Not that I had any doubts in prison about the rightness or correctness of it for me. In fact, maybe I have arrogance enough to assume that it has a relevance for a lot of other people; that it *is* a public necessity, in fact. I've

never had to do too much fumbling in that regard; yet at the same time I went through a dynamic of thought which thrust me more fully into the question of the meaning of prison—what can be accomplished there, what it does mean outside, what connection it has with the movement.

Q. *Do you find celibacy tougher in jail, or no tougher, or the same as out?*
A. It's tougher out. Because of the hypersexuality that's operating today, and the kind of sexual confusion that's operating in the peace movement, there are many more challenges outside, I would say, than if one were in jail, just single-mindedly going ahead with the business of trying to resist in some faint way, writing, or working with people. Outside it becomes much more difficult. Because in the oddest sort of way, movement people associate sexuality with humanity. But I'd like to stress that Dan and I feel that celibacy is crucial in the priesthood as an aid for revolutionary life style. We believe this very strongly, especially because we have made strong overtures to the other Christian communities in terms of action, in terms of awareness, political response, and all the rest, and gotten largely nowhere. With very, very good men. With men who have acted in a variety of ways in the past. And almost invariably the question of family obligations comes up, children, etc. So we feel celibacy can be a great freedom in a public forum.

Q. *Do you see prison in a sacramental sense—you know, in the old catechism definition of a sacrament being an occasion of grace? Is that how you see the example of your witness in prison?*
A. Yes. Being imprisoned for one's convictions is a Christian phenomenon above all, and also highly relevant politically. I would go so far as to say that if someone (not necessarily myself), if only one man were in prison for the right reasons,

although challenged by an entire country, it would still make a contribution of grace and new life in ways that cannot be imagined.

Q. *In your decision to go to jail and witness, are you saying that the central message of Christianity is redemption through the ultimate powerlessness of the crucifixion?*
A. Yes, most definitely. You have the example of Christ, and before that the whole prophetic experience of the Old Testament, and, of course, the Acts of the Apostles. Despite all the failures, there is a constant Christian tradition for two thousand years, leading to resistance to the Nazis, and more recently, the resistance against the French government during the Algerian crisis. For the committed Christian, there is a moral example, a religious guideline—almost a matter of doctrine. In addition, there is the political relevance of witnessing in jail, because there's not going to be basic change, there's not going to be human revolution—or even structural revolution in the sense that Bishop Helder Camara speaks of it—unless consciences are moved. And we don't know enough yet about how to move consciences, and this has its political aspect. And I've come to the conclusion that this can only be done by risk, by what people understand as suffering—what they are not willing to endure themselves. It can only be done by giving up one's freedom, which in a country like our own is only less precious than life itself. Americans have a phobia against jail because we have less of a tradition of resistance, and less of a tradition of jail experience influencing the national consciousness.

Q. *Let's speak a bit about Bonhoeffer, whose witness in jail has become a great example to many of us. Has it ever struck you that Bonhoeffer, within the very small nucleus of resistance in Germany, was in a small minority in pledging himself willing to kill Hitler himself? There were only about ten percent of the people involved in the*

*German resistance who were actually willing to commit
violence, and Bonhoeffer, the one eminent pastor in the
group, was one of the ten percent. How would you reflect
upon that, in terms of Christian nonviolence?*

A. I would say that this was the mistake of a very, very
good man who, because of the massiveness of the machine
against him, was led into desperation, and abandoned the
main premises of his own basic message by falling into this
trap. Bonhoeffer's example in this regard should be con-
trasted with that of another Protestant, Paul Schneider, who
died under Hitler and preserved intact the message of nonviolence right up to his death. To me, he is a greater man
than Bonhoeffer. I have read some of his statements, and
he was a man who had complete integrity to the end.

Q. *But aren't there times when religion is used as a front for
radical activity? What is the boundary line between being
religious and being radical? Do you sometimes use your
priesthood as a cover for radical activity?*

A. Well, wherever you are in this society, you're playing an
institutional role, and you have to deal with that fact. By
and large, you could say that you're always taking a political
position, regardless of intention. Some of the priests who
have resisted, and some of the young Catholics—like the
whole Catholic Worker crowd—they would emphasize their
institutional role out of fidelity not to what the Church is
institutionally, but what the Church ought to be as a Christian
community. You use the institutional role as a political platform in order to involve the Church in its own inherent contradictions, just as you would attempt to involve the society
in its own inherent contradictions. Politically, you can use the
Declaration of Independence against the system's contradictions. In the Church you use the Gospel against the institution,
or some of the declarations of Vatican II, or the Pope's
encyclical on development.

Q. *Then you would justify using the institution as a front or platform for your radical activity?*

A. You have no choice.

Q. *The paradox for so many of us is that people as radically free as you and your brother Dan should be so committed to this most totalitarian institution, the Catholic Church. Whereas people who are much more uptight on doctrine —people like Charles Davis—are the readiest to leave. Could you explain this paradox of your being free enough to feel ready to go to jail and witness, yet being determined to stay in the Catholic Church?*

A. There are many reasons. The first is that, although for at least sixteen centuries the Church has failed to make a full-hearted dedication to the Gospel, yet the Gospel is there. And the Gospel just may be the most perfect way of life that has been made available to mankind. That would be one reason.

The second reason would be that the Church will always exist as an institution, and it will always have the problem of coming to terms with the Gospel in a human fashion in its attempt to become a human community.

The third reason would be a historical understanding of the traditional hang-ups between church and state. The genesis of our whole trouble as institutional Catholics today is the alliance with the state, and being in reality a state-church. I would say that the ideal situation exists when the Church sees itself as a persecuted minority, not only when the state is explicitly totalitarian or fascist, but because the Church must always take upon itself the role of protest, must incorporate the whole prophetic dimension of a covenant with God. That is why the Church has the obligation to work for the moral purification of the social order. This necessarily involves challenging power as it becomes institutionalized, as power always does. If you accept the truth of Christ's teachings, particularly the death-life pattern mirrored in his passion and resurrection, and understand what that means in an existential way, then you have to be revolutionary, not only in your personal life but in public as well.

Q. *Could you expand on that? What does life after death mean to you, and what do you mean when you say you have to be revolutionary if you accept death the way Christ talked about it?*
A. What His death says to me is simply this: that He became most human in His death. And that it is the lot of men to become fully human in this way. Our humanity is not possible without having the closest possible relationship to God, and this relationship is not possible unless we undertake a process of sacrifice, of staying in the breach, of being with our brother in his agony. The crucifixion always spoke that way to me; our Lord achieved full humanity only when He died and sacrificed himself for the human family.

Q. *What do you mean by God? What is God to you?*
A. I still view God in largely conventional terms, as the Creator, the Father, as the end of our being and the great Protector of mankind, and the very lover of all of us, the great life force. But I don't philosophize very much about the idea of God.

Q. *What makes the Catholic Church unique to you? I ask that in view of the fact that powerlessness, nonviolence —all the things that mean so much to you—are equally central to Buddhism. What makes the message of Christianity unique to you?*
A. Simply this. There's no clear evidence for me that in the other great religions God has intervened in history to the point that He has in Christianity. To me, that's central. I believe very, very strongly in the fact that God did come

into our midst, He did fulfill a promise, the covenant is still in force. He taught us, and served us, and died for us. That makes Christianity relevant to me.

Q. *What does original sin mean to you? What is your notion of original sin?*

A. To me, it's largely the kind of antisocial weakness, providentially placed in all of us, that helps us—because it constitutes a challenge—to become human. And I really don't think that we would become human or would be able to measure up to any sort of ideal version or perception of volition if this challenge weren't within us. It constitutes an opportunity for man to transcend himself and become more than he is in the present, so much so that the future of man will be different.

Q. *How do you see the divinity of Jesus? In what sense was He divine?*

A. I am firmly convinced of the trinitarian understanding of the divine as an object of faith. And also of the incarnation. And I believe that God's revelation to us would be a very truncated, very superficial, and almost insulting thing if this were not verified by His Son taking our flesh and becoming man. I fear that I would be bowed down with hopelessness and frustration if I could not believe that. Because there would be so much less meaning to see in human life, or in my own, and a whole dimension of motivation would be absent. You see this verified in people who do not come from a Christian tradition and have no theology of the cross. It would seem that there are various psychic elements of emotional growth that have never come to life because they do not possess this resource.

Q. *How do you see death, and what comes after it?*

A. Well, I can't conceive, as Camus did, that our main object in life is to give expression to some version of human dignity, and that this is enough to keep a man going. I believe that human life means much more than that, that it is essentially spiritual, and that therefore it must have a continuity. And all the elements of revelation that I believe in substantiate that. I am not too much concerned with the "reward" aspect, the kind of heaven we've been traditionally taught. I believe that the future after death depends radically on what the person is *now*.

Q. *How do you explain the process whereby the revolutionary germs of the Christian faith have been suddenly liberated in our modern conscience?*

A. Probably the central factor in realizing some of our revolutionary roots is the international crisis. I'd like to think of Christians being motivated to a revolutionary stance because they believed in the Gospel, that this would be sufficient to bring them into the public forum as critics of public mores, particularly the mores of power. But this is not possible, and we have needed the Vietnamese struggle, the Cuban revolution, the crisis in Santo Domingo, the terrible suffering in Biafra, to teach us a great deal about revolution. This has forced us more and more to adopt a strictly revolutionary consciousness. And as the Church breaks up institutionally in all directions, and its very expensive walls fall of their own weight, there will be a more powerful nucleus of true Christians dedicated to a new Christian order, which does not mean they are interested in forming a new church.

Q. *Do you see the operation of the Holy Spirit in terms of a developing awareness among the poor and the dispossessed—their realization that it is not right that they are poor? This general awakening of the people to the wrongs of their plight—isn't that part of the awakening of the Church?*

A. Yes, man is really coming to a full self-consciousness, and the Church, because of technology and the communications that flow from technology, cannot avoid the implications of such a world event. As you say, an important part of this is the growing realization taking place in the Third World that the old pattern of destitution and hunger doesn't have to be anymore, that there are alternatives. This impinges upon the Church's consciousness, and of course when such an awareness confronts the institutional smugness, selfishness, passivity, alliance with power, and all the rest, the result is polarization. And you have a nucleus, waking up, and saying: Jesus Christ, what are you doing? Why does Forman have to appear at Riverside Church? Why does he have to go down and see Joe O'Brien in a back room of the New York Chancery Office? And what they mean is that the Holy Spirit is working through today's communication media and technology, making people aware of their wretched plight, and revolting against it.

Q. *At a recent Resistance conference people were running around wringing their hands, saying, "These Catholics, these Catholics," because of some dramatic actions, as in the case of the Baltimore Four, Catonsville Nine, and Milwaukee Fourteen, where you almost ask to be locked up. Do you consider such actions as a Catholic phenomenon?*

A. The people with whom I have acted realize that there is an immense reservoir of good in the Catholic Church. And if you leave it, you're automatically going to be involved in other institutions, unless you become a recluse. And the likelihood of forming substitute institutions is so highly hypothetical, maybe even ethereal. In their revolutionary activity they are aiming at a reform of conscience within the Church, as well as in society. Pope John used to speak about the Church's awareness of itself, and how central this was.

Well, if the Church was aware of itself, it would be forced into a whole new revolutionary dimension, and this would be worldwide. If the Church really had a realization of what the hell it is, it would be forced into continual reforming action.

However, it's certainly not a strictly Catholic phenomenon. Everything that's been done by groups like ours has been talked about within the Resistance and within the peace movement going back four or five years. I remember being in a think-tank at the University of Chicago where a lot of SDS graduates were talking about disruptive civil disobedience; the idea was so common at that level that when a person brought it up, people would begin to yawn. They'd gone over it too often already. It's not any special credit to us that we took it seriously; perhaps we had the preparation that *made* us take it seriously. And here I think that the Church has a unique contribution to make, simply because I don't find very many people, except Catholics, and a few rather unusual Resistance types, who do take it seriously, and who are willing to take it into the public forum and to test the national community by what they have done. There are the ones who are willing to say: Look, I'm not on trial, you are. There's no future for us or for you until we realize that. When you do, we'll be in a position of power, we'll constitute the majority, and change will come from that.

Q. *Let's return to your sense of the word "revolution." You use it differently from the way it's been used in the past, when it meant bloody uprising. What does the word mean to you in relationship to previous revolutions, like the American and the French revolutions?*

A. First of all, I must say that the term "revolution" as it is being employed by adherents of the Gospel and students of Gandhi means, on the human level—and this is the most natural thing—that people cannot develop until they change, that they cannot grow into humanity, they can't join the human race, unless they change. And change is revolution.

Q. *But why use this incendiary word for a nonviolent process that has never been associated with "revolution"?*
A. Simply because I don't think the word "revolution" can be avoided. One might encounter semantic difficulties in dealing with this because it's colored by so many different ideologies and moral fixations and emotional hang-ups, but it still remains a basic word, and when you break down its etymology it seems to have rather precise human connotations. Where are you going to find a substitute? One has to deal with it so that human connotations are made central. Otherwise, the whole dialogue concerning revolution—the whole dialectic, so to speak—lapses back into the historical bag, and we go on about revolution, the Bolshevik revolution, or the revolution in China in the late 1940's, and we get lost there, and end up talking about inevitability—the revolution of blood is a necessary historical process. The people who say that it is *not* inevitable are the only ones who, to my mind, understand revolution. In other words, the only ones who understand revolution are the ones who say that a nonviolent revolution is possible.

Q. *How do you foresee a nonviolent revolution in society? What alliances of social groupings in this country, for instance, would you visualize as possibly forming nonviolent revolution?*
A. It's very, very hard to say. Simply because the so-called Establishment, the structures of power, have been so resourceful up to the present time in resisting all the elements of nonviolent revolution, co-opting them and manipulating them, second-yessing them, in a sense anticipating them, no basic change has taken place. And this means that the imposition of violence is still very, very successful, nearly total,

and this in turn leads to real possibilities of violent reaction. But at any rate the student militant movement, in spite of the rhetoric, has operationally been nonviolent. For example, I don't see serious elements of violence at work on Cornell campus—from the student side, that is. There are large elements of psychological violence common to student militants, but it still has not resulted in overt violence.

Q. *Well, the blacks were armed with guns, loaded guns. How do you react to that?*
A. In the same way that I would react to North Vietnamese resisting our air onslaughts. A self-defensive measure. Football players in the white fraternities had brutalized black women at Cornell, and had threatened to march in to their dorms; the guns were symbolic defense. Existentially, I don't find any real quarrel with that; I feel it to be largely justified. Moreover, the guns weren't loaded.

Q. *During your testimony in Catonsville you stressed the fact that we Americans come from a revolutionary background. How would you differentiate the kind of revolution we had in this country in the eighteenth century from other revolutions—from the. French Revolution, and the Russian Revolution?*
A. Let's talk about the American Revolution first. We've had a lot of stupidities passed on to us in our classrooms about our revolution being some sort of ideal stereotype of revolution, which it wasn't at all. The revolution in this country was led by a nucleus of tradesmen, bankers, shippers, big shots who were uptight and furious about the imposition of economic control on their wealth by a foreign power. They knew the resources of this country. They knew its possibilities. And they didn't want foreign control, and they refused to submit to it. They led the nation into a fight for almost purely economic reasons. They had an awful lot of bona-fide reasons going for them, in terms of foreign domi-

nation, self-autonomy, self-determination, and so on, but it wasn't true revolution because it was an economic thing. It was an economic reshuffling rather than a true revolution.

Q. *Was the Russian Revolution a true revolution?*
A. No, it was not a true revolution, for different reasons. Mostly because of the elements of violence.

Q. *And how about the French Revolution?*
A. The French Revolution was not a real one either, by the very fact that it descended so quickly into an apotheosizing of bloodshed and murder.

Q. *You are denying the term "revolution" to the Russian experience; now are you also denying it to the French experience?*
A. Sure.

Q. *But then you're saying that there really never has been a revolution. That's your sense of the word, something that has not yet happened.*
A. Yes. And I would go beyond that, and say that, at least in the foreseeable future, there's not going to be a revolution. There's only going to be ongoing revolutions on the part of individuals and small groups.

Q. *"Uprisings"? Would that be a better way of putting it?*
A. Yes, "uprisings," or "moral rebellions," call it what you want. What I am trying to say is that if the planet is to be saved from real catastrophe, whether from nuclear war, or CBW or something like that, there has to be ongoing revolution all over, continuous revolution, as sort of a political constant.

Q. *In the Maoist sense?*
A. The Maoist experience has at least given us some sort of pattern for political revolution, although it has failed to provide guidelines for moral revolution—which to me is

really the key factor. It's not enough to challenge the bureaucracy which has entrenched itself; it's not enough to get the youth involved in the revolutionary process; one has to help people find themselves as people, and this means personal revolution projected into the social order, and tested there as to its valid elements. This is a way of saying that I can't be a man in this society unless I am in opposition to power. So, resistance is always synonymous with humanity, in my view.

Q. *Well, then, in your view, the only true revolution would be an anarchist revolution. Because the anarchist ideology is the only ideology in which political power is replaced by mutual aid.*

A. Right. Or, you can call it a new type of power. You can call it the type of power that would be dependent upon the original concept of service. In other words, a man's impact upon the community depends upon his qualifications for service. And the constant testing by the community of his service. You know: Are you for real? But the big need now, it would seem to me, is that power be engaged, that it be stalemated, shamed, and even excoriated in some instances, and condemned, and hopefully, reduced to impotence.

Q. *You have often referred to the draft-board raids as pre-revolutionary actions. And yet, in the past, this destruction of property always preceded violent uprisings. In what way do these symbolic raids fit into your scheme of revolution?*

A. Only in the most limited fashion. Yet, others say they were revolutionary acts in prerevolutionary times. But we have to be careful here; one thing needed in people who are attracted to this kind of activity is old-fashioned modesty. Whenever you make exaggerated claims about the dimensions of these affairs or their political effect, you immediately get caught in a whole series of traps. Because in terms of what power is doing in this country, such acts are very limited, almost childish in scope. When you stack the experience of the Resistance movement here against the resistance of the Vietnamese people, you begin to have a proper sense of proportion. It may well be that if we really understood what corporate power in this country is doing to the world, we wouldn't be operating on this level at all.

Q. *How would we be operating?*
A. I don't know. I would say that our imagination hasn't caught up with this reality at all. Hopefully, I would say that you would *not* be picking up a gun, but you would be doing something far more serious than attacking a draft board. Nevertheless, in terms of resistance against what power is doing, the draft-board raids are a highly symbolic and educative thing. And the price is not very great. Tom Lewis and I got a heavy sentence—six years. But we can appeal for reduction of sentence, and we can probably get it. And then our original six years will probably be chopped off to four, two and a half of which we'll serve. This isn't a heavy price in terms of what the realities of power are, or in terms of the suffering they cause elsewhere.